'I believe your book r...
the essence of what r...

Executive Master Alex Suh / 8th Degr...
World Kuk Sool Association, Texas, USA

'A brilliantly written book which packs
fascinating insights.'

Giovanni Soffietto / Founder & CEO
British Martial Arts & Boxing Association

'...touches on the very essence of why people
should practice and study martial arts.'

Master Martin Ducker / 7th Degree Black Belt
Kuk Sool Won, Halesworth, UK

'The book highlights the importance of
martial arts to many practitioners who
see it as a way of life.'

Sensei Jill Kelly / 6th Degree Black Belt
Ashington Shotokan Karate Club, UK

'A unique book. Quite different from other
types of martial art books.'

Master Barry Harmon / 9th Degree Black Belt
Kuk Sool Won, Clear Lake, Texas, USA

'Your book will make a huge difference
in the reader's understanding, experience
and pursuit of martial arts.'

Executive Master Alex Suh / 8th Degree Black Belt
World Kuk Sool Association, Texas, USA

'There are thousands of books on martial
arts, few cut through the noise and cliché
in such a succinct and intriguing way.'

Giovanni Soffietto / Founder & CEO
British Martial Arts & Boxing Association

'I'm very proud of Andrew, I think he's
a very clever boy.'

Margaret Stewart / 10th Degree Black Belt Mum

**WHY
EVERYTHING
YOU KNOW
ABOUT
MARTIAL
ARTS IS
WRONG***

This collection of stories includes themes of family, fear, fighting, faith and friendship... themes we all share, bound up in a book about martial arts.

I hope you discover or uncover something of value within the pages of this book.

**WHY EVERYTHING YOU KNOW ABOUT MARTIAL ARTS IS WRONG***

무술에 대해 아는 모든 것이 잘못된 이유*

**Dedicated to anyone brave enough to face a challenge that scares them.**

Compiled, written & designed by Andrew G Stewart
© Andrew G Stewart, 2021 / www.unbelievablebook.uk

**Vade Mecum:** A guide to be kept at hand for consultation.

**Second Edition / Softcover**

Typeset in Pembroke Light & Regular, Monday Semibold & London Semibold.

A catalogue record for this book is available from the British Library. ISBN 978-1-5272-8994-9
Published by The Unbelievable Book
Printed by Gipping Press Ltd. Suffolk IP6 8NZ

**Legal Disclaimer:** *Why Everything You Know About Martial Arts Is Wrong*™* is designed to offer a creative and personal perspective on matters of martial arts. This book aims to provide a range of ideas and perspectives on martial arts, but is not exhaustive in its coverage. The content of each article is the sole expression and opinion of the author. No warranties or guarantees are expressed or implied by the author, neither shall the author (and associates) be liable for any physical, medical, emotional, psychological, financial or commercial damages, including, but not limited to, special, incidental consequential or other damages. You remain responsible for your own choices, actions and the associated consequences. If that didn't sound very friendly, well, I'm sorry, it's the legal piece. The rest of the book is much friendlier :-)

'Everyone has a plan until they get punched in the mouth.' Mike Tyson

DGA
DAMN GOOD ADVICE

WHY
EVERYTHING
YOU KNOW
ABOUT
MARTIAL
ARTS IS
WRONG*

**WRONG HOW?** Martial arts make you invincible. Like Bruce Lee, you'll always defeat the bad guy and look super-cool doing it. You'll be bullet-proof, untouchable, unbeatable.

# WRONG*

*OK – you might look cool

*Why Everything You Know About Martial Arts Is Wrong\** aims to present the 'Why' behind martial arts.

This publication is not a technical guide or a history lesson. Neither is it a science and philosophy narrative designed to develop a warrior's mind. What you have in your hands is not exhaustive in its coverage, more a collection of first-hand accounts, stories, thoughts and personal observations – lightly held and humbly shared. I hope you enjoy reading this book as much as I have enjoyed creating it. →

Hello!

You might not give martial arts a second thought.

If that is you, this book has been written with you in mind and I'm genuinely delighted that you're reading it.

Now that we're together, let me ask you something: 'What do you think people 'get' from martial arts?' If you practise martial arts, ask yourself 'What do I actually receive?'

Your answers will vary – for some it might be about personal development, fitness and confidence. For others, a desire to improve technical skills to help fight better and defend more effectively. You might have elite combat skills, be a natural fighter destined for greatness. Or it might be about finding friendship, being part of a community or simply the act of learning something new. It might be an attempt to develop coping strategies, deal with conflict, stress or anxiety. It might be a back-up plan for when things don't go as hoped for or planned.

It might even be all of those things.

I'm a big believer that small changes can have a big impact on our lives, how we feel about ourselves, how we operate and function – our balance and health, both physically and mentally. Having thought about this for a while, I started to write. This publication represents some of those filtered thoughts. If you're pressed for time – here's my conclusion: I think it's not so much what you *get* from martial arts, I think it's more on the side of what you might achieve *with* martial arts. I believe that starts with the promise of possibility, a passionate sense of potential.

Your potential. →

# CONTENTS

12 Weird, Don't You Think?

18 Fight or Flight

22 A Load of Hong Kong Phooey

30 Art of the Empty Hand

42 Martial Arts Saved My Life

50 Fear Not

09 A Question

60 Fight Club

68 Interview with the Masters

76 Kuk Sool What?

Welcome to *Why Everything You Know About Martial Arts Is Wrong\**

First – the elephant in the room: not everything you know about martial arts is wrong. No one can punch faster than a speeding bullet (or catch one in their teeth), there's no such thing as the 'Dim Mak' or 'death touch' and it's unlikely that a martial artist can defeat five opponents all at once. I say unlikely, but you never know!

So what do we know, beyond what Hollywood and YouTube would have us believe? When it comes to martial arts, what's true, what's real and what's myth? How does what we hope to learn in the training hall apply to everyday life and what do people actually receive when they step into the dojang, dojo or training hall? Simple enough questions, although tricky to answer, yet that is the ambition behind this book, and the heart of it: to better present the 'Why' behind martial arts.

Second – when it comes to martial arts, who am I to write on such matters? While I hold a black belt in the Korean martial art of Kuk Sool Won™, I'm a novice. I'm neither crouching tiger nor hidden dragon, more an advanced beginner. However, I am a writer and designer by trade. For approaching three decades, I've helped people share stories in print and digital, where creativity has the ability to amplify and elevate people's voices and not just the ones that shout the loudest.

This publication has been created as a platform for some of those voices, echoed louder and captured permanently in print. You'll discover a life-saving story of courage and community and a sensational sum paid for a fight club. Closer to home you can read an interview with the masters and learn tactics for self-preservation. On a lighter note, we'll ask (and hopefully answer) the question: 'Isn't it all just a load of Hong Kong Phooey?'

As the world turns on its axis, we are facing unprecedented times. Ironic, as I write about martial arts (a system of combat designed for self-defence) the world has been brought to its knees by a fearful invisible enemy, COVID-19.[†]

In the case of COVID-19, a lack of preparedness contributed to the pandemic and ensuing pandemonium. Fear travelled fast along digital highways. What followed was a loss of routine and purpose, a loss of connection and experiences, the rituals of life. Loss of jobs and income, the loss of health and loved ones. In the words of Val Uchendu, 'Loss is like a wind, it either carries you to a new destination or it traps you in an ocean of stagnation. You must quickly learn how to navigate the sail, for stagnation is death.'

But perhaps all is not lost.

There are times in life when a degree of fear isn't always unwelcome if it encourages people to adopt behaviours that might reduce levels of chaos and anxiety, preserve life and limit loss. To prepare for a tough season, where we might learn to cope or somehow accept loss. In the words of German philosopher Arthur Schopenhauer 'It is loss which teaches us about the worth of things.'

I hope you find this first collection of stories worthy of your time. That each story might encourage you to defend against the hesitant voice of doubt, overcome obstacles, counter with courage and buttress belief in yourself.

By paring back and making space, it might just ignite a sense of possibility and potential to manifest positive change – where each of us has a chance not only to put ourselves back together, but also – maybe – even our world.

**Andrew G Stewart**
JKN (1st Dahn) Kuk Sool Won™

†COVID-19, a devastating illness caused by the corona virus.

Let me ask
you something.

When you think of
martial arts, who
springs to mind?

I bet I know
the answer...

# ...this guy.

**Bruce Lee →**

As if he needs introducing. A philosophy major at Washington University. That's not what made him famous – that was Kung Fu Fighting and teaching. A cultural phenomenon, founder of Jeet Kune Do (translates: The Way of the Intercepting Fist), movie star and legend. When it comes to martial arts, the enduring legacy of Bruce Lee *is* martial arts.

Different can be misinterpreted and badged weird,
but weird can also be surprising and mysterious.

# WEIRD, DON'T' YOU THINK?

Words: Andrew G Stewart
Pictures: Keagan Henman on Unsplash

WHY
EVERYTHING
YOU KNOW
ABOUT
MARTIAL
ARTS IS
WRONG*

天官賜酒

# People don't fit the standard model, because there isn't a standard model. People are different. We all sit outside the general rule of 'normal' – what ever normal actually means.

After you kicked it or hit it, you might have discovered that the ball didn't go in the intended direction – and sometimes we're picked last in the line-up. It turns out that we're not all cut out for team sports like football or rugby, cricket or hockey. We're different. Although some people are similar, divisions do occur. It can cause tension between those who can and those who can't, those who do and those who don't. But different makes us interesting, it enriches the mix, don't you think? Differences can unite us, but they can also divide us. To be left out can mean you miss out – miss out on acceptance, adventures, acknowledgement, friendship and fun. Not because you're weird, just different. Different can be misinterpreted and badged weird, but weird can also be surprising and mysterious. And there it is: the two 'M's: mystery and martial arts, a connection which when investigated may prove to be well founded, even true!

So what do people really know about martial arts? Wipe on, wipe off, wax on, wax off, if you're familiar with the 1984 film *Karate Kid*, where Mr Miyagi (pictured), a martial arts master (also an unassuming repairman) attempts to teach Daniel LaRusso Karate. It's the Hollywood lens through which many of us view and determine the value and utility of martial arts. The film's narratives play on themes of mystery rather than clarity.

Clarity has a tendency to get to the point. Despite its opacity, mystery sometimes has a part to play. It tempts us, gives us hope and helps us deal with the things we don't fully understand, like faith and belief; and whatever you believe, hope sits there in the shadows, it's there to help get us through. On the mysteries of martial arts, if Karate is the 'art of the empty hand', clarity is the art of simplicity – it's easy, sincere, honest and practical. Mystery brings intrigue that is enticing. At times, it can ask us to work a little harder, be a bit braver and dive into the unknown. In the interests of clarity, let me say this book is a proclamation and declaration about martial arts.

This publication is also a handbook for the new recruit, the volunteer, supporter and teacher. It is a point of ready reference for the founder and first-timer. It is also about legacy and choice, where we might challenge the status quo to see if things can be done differently or perhaps more effectively. For some, that might be about engagement, first with ourselves, then maybe with others. Like any relationship, it might be less about asking 'What can I get from martial arts?' More on the side of 'What can I achieve with martial arts?' To appreciate the difference. Then, if you take part, benefit from the value of the relational exchange. →

↑ Mr Miyagi, Karate Kid, 1984
→ Weird, don't you think?

Differences can unite us, but they can also divide us. To be left out can mean you miss out – miss out on acceptance, adventures, acknowledgement, friendship and fun. Not because you're weird, just different.

On themes of value, in particular the merit and worth of reading, it was Epictetus, the Greek philosopher (born a slave) who said 'Books are the training weights of the mind.' A powerful aphorism, you could say a truth that captures the spirit and benefits of martial arts, which for many are less about prevailing against an enemy, more about finessing a sequence of movements and techniques – where we have a chance to cultivate both the mind and body.

When it comes to reading, you're likely the best judge of what is and isn't of value. As the author of this narrative, I hope that you find something of worth and utility in some of the stories within. For what it's worth, creating this publication has certainly helped me order my scattered thoughts, in an attempt to make sense of what I receive from martial arts. Thoughts captured, conclusions drawn, I then thought 'Maybe it might help someone else?' 'Maybe' then turned into this thing that you now hold in your hands – an attempt to shed light and provide some clarity around the mystery of martial arts.

The writer Franz Kafka suggests 'A book should be an ice-axe to break the frozen seas within us.' I like that, and while this book is no ice-axe, I would encourage you to read and experience some of the themes within, then decide its value and role in your life, your context. If you are reading this book, you have already started on a pathway designed to better present what you might receive when it comes to the matters and misgivings of martial arts. This narrative is a small part of a continuous process of change, and success lies not so much in the experience of reading and turning the pages, the hinge lies in your individual response to the prompts and suggestions contained within it. Perhaps recognition and change of a previously held view, a change in a bias or belief. Perhaps a review of the way martial arts might be of value and benefit, even utility in the place you find yourself. I think you have an appetite for ambition and a capacity for change. That may result in a commitment to train, to staying the course or writing a plan. That might fill you with angst or manifest malaise, and change, at times may require others to support, guide and help you realise a particular ambition.

In a few lines, this story is a catalyst designed to prod and provoke, a call to precipitate action. To achieve anything of worth takes buy-in, ownership and time. This is not about fighting like Bruce, becoming a celebrity fighter, winning world titles or becoming notorious, it's about re-framing the old and reclaiming the new, the different and maybe even the weird. It (almost) goes without saying, that martial arts might at times appear a bit weird, but it is for anyone, just not everyone. Truth is, we're all a bit weird, some of us are half-crazy. But that makes for a more interesting life... Don't you think? △

## 'Think about your legacy because you are writing it every day.'

Gary Vaynerchuk, Entrepreneur

For many, the benefit of martial arts is less about prevailing against an enemy, it's more about finessing a sequence of movements and techniques – where we have a chance to cultivate both the mind and body.

Fight or flight to know the difference
Might just lead to your deliverance
Before the anger ignites to blaze
From alley ways out from malaise

Ambushed by fear you feel the weight
It's not the time to placate
No time to dally choose your fate
Despite the fear you can vacate

Sense the danger hem you in
Control your courage, breathe within
Invite the exit then the win
Before the chaos can begin

Take flight not fight on this night
Another time it's might that's right
For now the distance is in play
There might just be another way

To sense that calm is close at hand
Make haste embrace the hinterland
To live to fight another day
Take the chance, get on your way

*Andrew G Stewart*

*To everything there is a season,
and a time to every purpose under the
heaven: a time to be silent and a time to
speak, a time to love and a time to hate,
a time for war and a time for peace.
Ecclesiastes 1: 7, 8.*

'Home Sweet Home'
Mixed Media Sculpture (detail)
Artist: Sam Stewart

JUST RUN

Phooey, hooey, nonsense and silly. Words that describe Penrod Pooch, aka 'Hong Kong Phooey' the martial art vigilante cartoon crime-fighter.

# A LOAD OF HONG KONG PHOOEY

Real deal or just martial arts mockery?

Words: Andrew G Stewart
Pictures: Unsplash/commissioned + private collection

WHY
EVERYTHING
YOU KNOW
ABOUT
MARTIAL
ARTS IS
WRONG*

# Against a surge of martial art fads, Hong Kong Phooey hit the small screens in the mid-1970s. A spoof of the Kung Fu craze. So what's changed?

It was the 1970s. John Travolta took to the dance floor in the world's most famous (polyester) white suit, Farrah Fawcett became a Charlie's Angel and ABBA took 'Scandi cool' to another level. There was a major cultural craze for Asian martial arts both in the movies and on the small screen. R&B singer Carl Douglas got everybody 'Kung Fu Fighting', Kwai Chang Caine aka David Carradine starred in the long running series *Kung Fu* and the film *Enter the Dragon*, starring Bruce Lee, was a box office smash. It was also the debut of the cartoon character Hong Kong Phooey, 'The number one super guy'. A little known masked martial arts hero devised by Hanna-Barbera Productions for the ABC network. Hong Kong Phooey, the secret identity of Penrod Pooch, a 'mild-mannered' police janitor who worked under the watchful eye of Sergeant Flint and police dispatcher Rosemary. Hong Kong Phooey, the canine crusader, was assisted by his striped feline partner Spot and fought crime by using his martial arts skills. Whilst Penrod believed in the power of kung fu (regularly consulting his martial arts handbook, mid-fight) it was in fact Spot, his sidekick cat who regularly saved the day.

As a kid growing up in the suburbs of Birmingham in the 1970s, Jackanory, Blue Peter and John Craven's Newsround preceded 30 minutes of Phooey action. It was a cartoon that characterized a simpler time, where on-demand content and YouTube was as distant as flying cars. A time when Spangles and long summers,

The Dukes of Hazzard, boredom and BMX bikes ruled the world. I miss those days. But don't most of us look back on our childhoods with a mixture of blurred nostalgia, sharp colours and in my case, knitted men's tank tops? Childhood, like the TV we watched was experienced in low-resolution.

Hong Kong Phooey not only spoofed the Kung-Fu movie craze, it was also a parody of the cop shows of the same era, like CHiPs, Hawaii Five-O and Columbo. Where buffoon-like antics reinforced the perception that martial arts, when applied to real world situations verged on the laughable. Humour played on predictable gags and incompetence, where Hong Kong Phooey (transported by his 'Phooeymobile') would blunder into situations, and against all the odds, win the day. Unsurprisingly, the series lasted only 16 episodes, from September 7 to December 21 1974. Hong Kong Phooey didn't know Kung Fu and the storylines were a little unimaginative. It was not the most memorable cartoon series of all time. The likes of Charlie Brown, Snoopy, Bugs Bunny and Scooby Doo have fared far better. But we can't really blame poor Penrod. After all, it was the scriptwriters who called the shots. Through the lens of nostalgia, like many of the cartoons of the time, they were products of the era. Where cultural stereotypes crept into the art, storylines and caricatures. Although important not to lose sight of the role of the cartoon. In many cases, designed to lampoon the ludicrous, parody the pompous or just plain entertain. →

→ Yes, I own a copy of 'Kung Fu Fighting'. Released as a single in 1974, at the height of the chopsocky (martial art) film craze. The single rose to the top of the British, Australian, Canadian and American charts. Although contrary to popular belief, not everybody was kung fu fighting.

→ 'Monkey Magic' by Japanese rock band Godiego. From the cult Japanese TV show 'Monkey' aired in the U.K. in the late 1970s. A motley crew, led by the immortal Monkey, tasked to protect the monk Tripitaka on his (although it was really a 'her', the beautiful actress Masako Natsume) quest to retrieve some holy scriptures. Loved watching this with my twin sister Naomi.

The legacy of Hong Kong Phooey, his antics and double life as a martial arts crime fighter sit in the shadows when compared to legitimate stars like Chuck Norris and Bruce Lee. Although each were contributors and pioneers in the action movie genre, it was the latter that set a trajectory and platform for the likes of Jean Claude Van Damme, Jet Li, Tony Jaa and Jackie Chan. More recently, high-profile actors including Keanu Reeves, Michael Jai White, Scott Adkins and Jason Statham. Modern-day antiheros, known for their action-thriller roles, martial art skills and machiavellian characters who blur the edges between what is and isn't possible. It was the poet Samuel Taylor Coleridge who coined the term 'suspension of disbelief' back in 1817. A suggestion that we believe, or more accurately, feel that what we are viewing is actually happening. Reality is paused. We lose ourselves in the action, transported out of our seats and into an alternative reality. We believe in the super-human speed, strength and agility of the martial art hero. Where a fusion of wire-fu (a combination of wire work and kung fu) and post-production wizardry, captures a moment in time. Also the character, who appears frozen mid-air, while the camera circles the action.

In many cases, martial art movies of the modern era have bridged the divide between eastern philosophy and heritage and western sensibilities. Although storylines often share parallels, a familiar rubric: the lead character, a humble hero and martial-art expert experiences an injustice. This event ignites a mission to right a wrong. Along a perilous journey, the hero meets wise men and courageous allies, then enters a martial arts competition. A dramatic final battle ensues, despite early set-backs, the hero is victorious and saves the day. The End. Roll credits. They are stories with themes of honour, redemption, revenge, survival and in some cases salvation. Films like *Enter the Dragon*, *Fists of Fury*, *The Matrix*, *Undisputed* and *John Wick*.

*The Karate Kid* film, first released back in 1984 is probably one of the best known martial art movies of all time. It proved popular, realising over $90 million at the box office, ranking number 5 in the top grossing movies of 1984. Ghostbusters was #1, in case you wondered. So why did the film do so well? I believe it was because the film was rooted in themes that we can all relate to, like love, hope, fear, longing, loyalty, wonder and trust. We all like stories of trust and hope, because we can all relate to a message of optimism in the face of adversity. In the case of Daniel LaRusso, the karate kid, he was the new kid in town who fell for a local girl. He was bullied by a bunch of karate students, until Mr Miyagi taught Danny the power of karate. In the words of Ralph Macchio, the actor who played Daniel LaRusso 'The film and the character just struck a chord back in the day,' Macchio says. 'Daniel LaRusso, he was every kid next door. I think that's part of what connected. He had no business winning anything, so we all could be that kid. We all were that kid who was navigating adolescences, that kid who might have felt like the outsider in a new town, the fish-out-of-water, the child of a single parent, or was bullied… all these things that we all brush up against as we navigate adolescence. They're very human elements to life and I think that's part of what worked with that character and why he became such an inspirational character and why the movie caught on.'

Like so many stories and themes, they connect us, inspire action and at times they can change our perceptions. Stories can also be a catalyst that compel us to take a stand, make a commitment and maybe even join a martial arts club. Take the film *Kick Boxer* starring Jean-Claude Van Damme. It was the film that stepped 6TH Dahn Paul Taylor into searching for his inner Bruce Lee. You can read his story on page 68. Films can catapult us into a different future, where we have a chance to be the hero, like Hong Kong Phooey. You never know, you might even save the day. △

# 'Reality is paused. We lose ourselves in the action, transported out of our seats and into an alternative reality.'

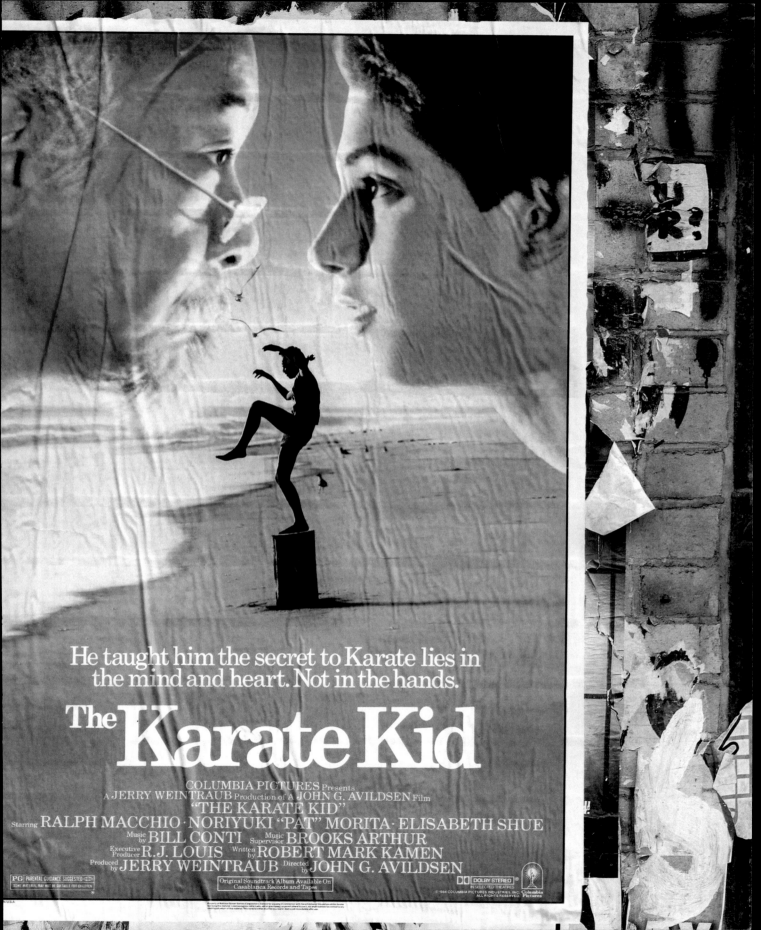

**LESSON #1: SITUATIONAL AWARENESS**
TRY NOT TO BE IN THE WRONG PLACE AT THE WRONG TIME

FOR INSIGHTS ON MARTIAL ARTS, CHECK OUT
RAMSEY 'COACH' DEWEY'S YOUTUBE CHANNEL:

▶ **RAMSEY DEWEY**

NOTHING IS
GOOD FOR
THE STREETS
NOW GET
OUT THERE
AND TRAIN

Ramsey L. Dewey

Undefeated Street Fighter*

*By avoiding the streetfight

DGA

**Beyond the movies, the myths and the manly men's aftershave 'Hai Karate', what's the draw and the story behind the modern-day art of the empty hand?**

# KARATE

Back in the late 1960s, a new aftershave came on to the market. Called 'Hai Karate', the budget cologne came with a warning 'Use too much and you're asking for trouble.' The aftershave included an essential self-defence guide, describing the cologne as a 'lethal weapon' against the opposite sex. A line that was dropped on the final leaflet. The aftershave proved popular at the time with a sketchy claim: *One whiff and you become irresistible – it drives women out of their minds.* It played to the stereotype of the age, a product of its time. In retrospect, the marketing and advertising shouldn't be judged too harshly.

Memorable advertising usually has a spark of truth somewhere in the sales pitch. Certain smells have been considered aphrodisiacs way before Hai Karate was splashed all over. That an aftershave makes you 'irresistible' is hardly a truthful presentation of a perfume, or a new one. It probably just smells like nostalgia now, but it might have given you a bit of courage. After all, we've all bought into the catchy marketing slogans 'Because I'm Worth It' or we've chosen to 'Just Do It'. Strap lines espoused by L'Oréal and Nike, designed to convince us, the consumers, to buy their product over the competition. We buy into the promises, even though on closer inspection, we suspect the slogans are just salesy claptrap.

Like like so many forms of advertising, there is a kernel of truth. Take Hai Karate: *Be careful how you use it.* It's true. If you're a martial artist, you'll know that. My martial arts journey started with karate, the martial art, not the manly men's aftershave. About a million years ago, I graded under Sensei Frank Brennan, an elite competitor, now a highly respected 8th Dahn Shotokan instructor. Also a technical instructor and coach at Karate Union Great Britain (KUGB). Back then, I caught a scent of Sensei Brennan's passion and commitment for karate. It was an experience I never forgot. This feature and this book are a celebration of people like Sensei Brennan who have dedicated their lives to martial arts. A testimony to the commitment of mentors and students, both past and present. It's also important not to forget the role of countless parents and guardians. People who have sat on chairs at the edge of halls, watching their children. I often think they deserve a special certificate, a belt and a round of applause. Recognition of their encouragement and time spent watching patiently from the sidelines. That's a special sort of commitment, don't you think? This feature on karate is an attempt to capture that sense of family, as well as present a narrative around the past, present and future role of karate. ➔

Words: Andrew G Stewart
Pictures: Xavier Servolle / Kphotos.net
Ashington Shotokan Karate, Karate Union of Great Britain

## WHY EVERYTHING YOU KNOW ABOUT MARTIAL ARTS IS WRONG*

Sensei Jill Kelly with Sensei Keinosuke Enoeda and Sensei Andy Sherry after passing her 4th Dan grading

Sensei Frank Brennan scoring with ushiro geri in competition kumite early 1970's

Sensei Frank Brennan scoring with mawashi geri at the KUGB National Championships around 1983

↑ Picture credits: Special thanks to Sensei Jill Kelly (6th Dan); Dylan ... Karate Club & KUGB

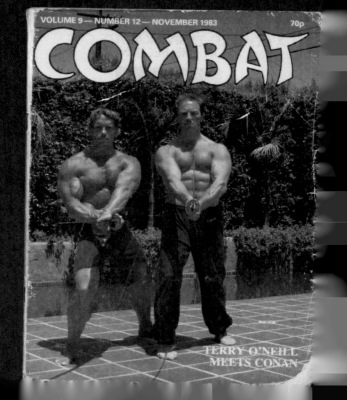

VOLUME 9 — NUMBER 12 — NOVEMBER 1983    70p

# COMBAT

TERRY O'NEILL
MEETS CONAN

# Could 'one word' capture the centuries of tradition, culture, history and ceremony associated with martial arts? That starts with a search...

If you type 'martial arts' into Google, you will discover over 55 million videos. That's a lot of footage to get through, from the frankly bizarre to the hands-on and instructional. Like the video by Michael J White, a martial artist and Hollywood actor who demonstrates 'How to strike with maximum power.' According to Michael, it's a straight right, reverse punch, or in karate parlance, a Gyaku-zuki – in case you were wondering.[1] It's tricky to define martial arts. There are so many angles, views and expressions, with over 180 martial arts styles on offer.[2] From A to Z, Aikido to the centuries-old tradition of Zulu Stick Fighting. That doesn't even include Karate's sub-categories like Shotokan, Kyokushin or Wado-Ryu. To define martial arts, in a word, is a bit like trying to catch smoke, an impossible task. Or is it? Even a blind squirrel finds a nut once in a while!

So here goes. A search for one word that captures the centuries of tradition, culture, history and ceremony associated with martial arts. In a word, Karate. A word that conjures an almost visible, animated expression of what martial arts represents. A word that transcends its literal definition, karate has become a touchstone that connects the past and present-day worlds of martial arts. Karate captures a spirit that for millions of people *is* martial arts. And it's popular. Around 100 million people on five continents and in 192 countries practise karate.[3] That's a heck of a lot of kicking and punching going on. But karate goes way beyond just kicking and punching. I think we both know that. But what does karate actually mean? Take the word 'karate'. It's a combination of two Chinese characters: *kara*, meaning empty, and *te*, meaning hand. It's literally the art of the 'Empty Hand'. It's one lens through which to view the martial art. Although for many, karate is more a philosophy, an approach to life that forms a strong foundation. In the words of Kenwa Mabuni, one of the first practitioners to teach karate on mainland Japan, 'Karate-do is a lifetime study.' *Karate-do* translates 'The Way of the Empty Hand.' So there it is. Karate is a way of life. That's it. Job done. You can stop reading now.

But don't stop reading. That's just a starting point, a headline to a far bigger story, a narrative that this book hopes to capture and unpack – the 'why' behind martial arts. If you practise martial arts, you'll know participation is less on the side of preservation with a destination in mind. It's more on the side of a continuous journey, where, over time, you hope to develop and improve, both in competencies as well as character. There's also a convergence, where your story folds into an altogether bigger story. One that's part of a legacy. As well as our present-day masters and teachers, each of us who practise and participate in martial arts have a role to play: to continue that legacy, set down by the founding fathers centuries ago. It's what keeps martial arts alive. Over generations, a progressive cause that brings us together and unites us under one banner. To consider the present and future role of karate, it sometimes pays to see where we've been. A brief pause in the proceedings, as we glance in the rear-view mirror. I'd like to invite you on a journey to the past. ➔

Japan's Arata Kinjo lands the kick in the Senior Team Male Kata – final bout. Photo taken during World Championship Madrid 11 November 2018. Photo © Xavier Servolle / Kphotos.net

We start our mini-adventure back in the late 19th century, on a Japanese island that sits on the edge of the East China Sea. Picture yourself on the largest of the Ryukyu Islands, modern-day Okinawa, a Japanese island, just under 1,000 miles from Tokyo. It's Wednesday, martial art training day in the local hall. Sensei Anko Itosu, considered by many to be the founding father of modern karate, is in the hall. Master Anko is instructing one of his students, Sensei Gichin Funakoshi, founder of Shotokan karate.[4] Right there in front of you are the mentor and his student, engaged in the act of teaching and training. As each movement unfolds to the next, together they are laying down the foundation of a new martial art. An evolution of what has passed previously. A living story, passing from one person to another; and while so much has changed over time, the story of karate remains. Where a particular style of martial art is passed on from mentor to student, in the time-honoured tradition. One movement at a time, one person to another. Fast forward to 1955, when Sensei Gichin Funakoshi founded the *Japanese Karate Association* (JKA). Through Sensei Funakoshi's senior students, Shotokan karate has evolved into one of the world's most popular martial arts.

It's generally accepted that there are four major styles of karate in Japan: Shito-Ryu, Goju-Ryu, Wado-Ryu and Shotokan.[5] If you're wondering what the names mean, take Wado-Ryu. 'Wa' meaning peace or harmony, 'do' meaning way or path; 'Ryu' simply means style. Each style is under the banner of karate, although nuanced differences distinguish one from the other: height of stances, focus on speed over power, counter-striking as well as evasion, absorption, deflection and projection techniques. If you described yourself as a 'karatekas', a practitioner of karate, you'll be familiar with this next bit. If you're new to martial arts, or just starting out – here's a few basics. Karate is predominantly a striking art, when compared to the more fluid, circular movements of say Kung Fu. Karate is a 'hard' style, characterized by meeting force with force, as opposed to a 'soft' style, enacted by deflecting

force and momentum, characterized by Kung Fu and Kuk Sool Won, the Korean martial art. Karate is more linear. Incorporating punching, kicking knee and elbow strikes, as well as open-handed techniques. Full-contact, semi-contact and light-contact, over 24 styles have evolved over time,[6] including the world's most popular: Shotokan.[7] Shotokan is more of a hard martial arts style, due in part to the emphasis on high-impact strikes, long stances and sparring techniques. When it comes to practice, karate is divided into three parts: Kihon, Katas and Kumite. Kihon is a Japanese term meaning 'basic fundamentals', with a focus on stances, blocks, punches, strikes and kicks. Katas are pre-arranged forms of simulated combat, incorporating Kihon elements in combination. The sequence of connected movement promotes memory, both in the mind and muscles, developing strength, rhythm and power. If you're a student of Shotokan, you might remember the *Gohon Kumite*, a five- step sparring training drill with a focus on punching and blocking. The ambition is to fine-tune motor skills, to be executed without thought. To complete the trio, Kumite is the application of Kihon and Kata in context – sparring, the fight scenario in real time.

Karate, like so many martial arts, is about personal advancement, where we have an opportunity to cultivate the mind and the body. As well as a form of self-defence, participation is an opportunity to develop resilience, improve physical fitness, confidence and self-esteem. A chance to develop self-defence techniques, improve coping strategies or a sense of agency, where friendship, community and having fun all feature. When it comes to karate, competition is part of the culture. Where techniques and tactics are put to the test. An opportunity to apply competencies and capabilities, skills and stamina. The hope – a podium finish (more on that later), maybe a win, to be magnanimous in victory or learn humility in defeat, where we hope to improve from the trials of combat. A place that forges character, courage and patience. ➔

# 'The ultimate aim of karate lies not in victory nor defeat, but in the perfection of the character of its participants.'

Gichin Funakoshi, founder of Shotokan karate

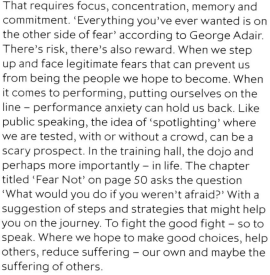

'A kata is not fixed or immoveable. Like water, it's ever changing and fits itself to the shape of the vessel containing it. However, kata are not some kind of beautiful competitive dance, but a grand martial art of self-defense – which determines life and death.'

Kenwa Mabuni, Karateka

沖縄

That requires focus, concentration, memory and commitment. 'Everything you've ever wanted is on the other side of fear' according to George Adair. There's risk, there's also reward. When we step up and face legitimate fears that can prevent us from being the people we hope to become. When it comes to performing, putting ourselves on the line – performance anxiety can hold us back. Like public speaking, the idea of 'spotlighting' where we are tested, with or without a crowd, can be a scary prospect. In the training hall, the dojo and perhaps more importantly – in life. The chapter titled 'Fear Not' on page 50 asks the question 'What would you do if you weren't afraid?' With a suggestion of steps and strategies that might help you on the journey. To fight the good fight – so to speak. Where we hope to make good choices, help others, reduce suffering – our own and maybe the suffering of others.

When it comes to karate and competition, you've got two types: Kata and Kumite. Unlike Mixed Martial Arts (MMA), sparring in karate (Kumite) is more on the side of points-based scoring than submission or knock out. Not exclusively though. Full-contact karate, like Kyokushin, advocates full-force sparring, where the victor gets ahead on points or gets a knock out. Not for the 'feint' hearted. In the feature 'Fight Club' on page 60, you can read about the billionaire business of brawling. A world dominated by the fight promoters Ultimate Fighting Championship (UFC). A highly-curated mixed martial art (MMA) fight experience, which has exploded onto the fight scene in recent years. MMA combat perhaps answers the age-old questions 'What's the best, most effective form of martial art?' The answer, according to combat coach Ramsey Dewey, centres on a blended approach. Where any number of 'systems' combine to take down the opponent. A fusion of martial arts disciplines, with the exception of Zulu Stick Fighting. And there are some exceptional fighters, including the Canadian 'Hall of Famer' Georges St Pierre. He had a foundation in karate, before adding Muay Thai and Brazilian Jiu Jitsu. →

↖ Ryukyu Islands from the air; part of the Miyako Islands, Japan's Okinawa Prefecture.
← Hand brush written Kanji (logographic Chinese/Japanese characters used in the Japanese writing system) character of 'Okinawa prefecture'.

Georges St Pierre (GSP) holds a black belt in both Kyokushin karate and Brazilian Jiu Jitsu. To broaden his repertoire, he took boxing and wrestling lessons, but his foundation was karate. That's where it started. Another MMA fighter, Lyoto Machida, a Brazilian professional mixed martial artist and karateka, has proved the effectiveness of karate as a combat sport. Back in 2014, in an article published by the Bleacher Report (a website focused on sport and sport's culture), Jack Slack talked about Lyoto Machida. How tournament karate is evident in Machida's striking style. To transition into MMA, both GSP and Lyoto Machida understood the benefit of other martial art systems, the blended approach that includes karate, to great effect. You've got to learn to box, have fast hands, quick movements, use angles. Interestingly, in Machida's last win, hosted by the American MMA fight promoters Bellator, it was a flying knee and a series of punches that finished off his opponent Chael Sonnen with a TKO. A tough and accomplished fighter, Chael talked about how quickly Machida closed down the space, of his elusiveness. Chael Sonnen retired after the fight. In the moving post-fight press conference he stated 'Everything was going my way, until it wasn't.' Isn't that life, in a few words? In his final post-fight press conference, Chael was celebrated for his commitment, courage and contribution.

It was Sir Ernest Shackleton, the polar explorer, who said 'Optimism is true moral courage.' When it comes to competing, optimism is a useful tool, where self-belief is a vision of victory. At the very least, optimism is a mindset that suggests there is opportunity when faced with difficulties. When we compete, it's the taking part that counts. Or is it? The father of the modern Olympic Games, Baron Pierre de Coubertin said 'The most important thing in the Olympic Games is not winning but taking part; the essential thing in life is not conquering but fighting well.' Perseverance, hard work and sacrifice, striving to beat a personal best as well as going for gold. The medals, well, maybe they just underline a more valuable lesson – what we might discover about ourselves on the path of the hero's journey. On Thursday, August 5th 2021, karate makes its first appearance in an Olympic Games: Tokyo 2020, delayed a year due to the Covid pandemic. Karate joins judo and Taekwondo, inducted into the Olympics in 1964 and the year 2000 respectively. Three days of competition will determine the first-ever Olympic champions. Who will become the first karateka Olympians in history? Spanish karatekas Sandra Sanchez and Damian Quintero won gold and silver respectively at the 2020 World Championships. Both will be going for Gold in Tokyo. All the action will unfold at the Nippon Budokan (Martial Arts Hall). Known as the spiritual home of Japanese martial arts, the Nippon Budokan is located in the district of Chiyoda, in the centre of Tokyo, very close to the Imperial Palace. Can you imagine what it would feel like to compete in that arena? A convergence of the past, present and future worlds of karate. I wonder what Sensei Anko Itosu would make of it? One thing's for sure, an international platform will no doubt raise awareness, also add prestige and recognition to karate. Sponsorship and associated funding will likely catapult gifted practitioners into the world of the professional athlete. For the likes of the local karate club, it may encourage support at a grassroots level, which has to be a good thing. Although the Olympic inclusion may dial down an aspect of karate, in so far as standardising rules, when it comes to kumite and kata events. Techniques that have developed to provide self defence in the first, the proposed points-based 'light' or 'no contact' rules will require a recalibration of audience expectations when compared to full contact styles like Kyokushin or MMA. It's perhaps important to remember that in all forms of curated combat, rules exist at some level. For example, you're not allowed to poke your opponent in the eye in MMA. Context and application. Real world self-defence scenarios and points-based competition – as different as tap and ballroom dancing. I think there's a place for all forms of martial arts, where the tenets of respect, humility, perseverance are central. Whether you're going for Gold in Tokyo, training in your local club's dojo or toe to toe in the MMA Octagon. Olympic karate is just one expression, an exciting new chapter in the ongoing story of karate. →

## 'Knowing is not enough; we must apply. Willing is not enough; we must do.'

Bruce Lee

There's a video on the KUGB website, an epitaph to Sensei Enoeda, a Japanese master of Shotokan karate (also a former Chief Instructor of the KUGB). In the video, senior instructor Sensei Terry O'Neil, himself a highly competent and experienced Shotokan practitioner, talks about a lifetime of memories. How Sensei Enoeda was like a father to him, for most of his adult life. There's a lament to Sensei O'Neil's reflections, although an overwhelming sense of celebration. Like Sensei O'Neil, this book and my story would look quite different in the absence of past instructors. Like Sensei Frank Brennan as well as my modern-day Kuk Sool Won mentors and teachers. There will be people in your life who've played a part in shaping and determining the person you are today. Sometimes the people who influence and guide us on our journey never get to hear about the role they played. Like the rudder on a ship, they contribute to both our direction and destination in life. It's important not to forget the difference we can make in the lives of others. The role we play, the things we say and do (and choose not to do). Words can be bullets or seeds, according to author Gary Chapman. They can build us up or take us down. Plant the truth and it has a chance to take root and grow, maybe even flourish.

This feature started with a search for one particular word that hoped to capture the centuries of tradition, culture, history and ceremony of martial arts. A global movement centred on self improvement; like a country, owned by no one, it belongs to everyone. When it comes to describing the enduring spirit that sits at the very heart of the art of the empty hand, karate is not the so much the last word, but the first. △

↗ From the archives. Can you see the poster behind Sensei Enoeda? Line one reads: Cultivate the spirit of perseverance. Some statements are universal and timeless.

Ashington Shotokan Karate Club students with Sensei Andy Sherry, 9th Dan after being selected onto the KUGB England Kata Squad in 2020 less than two months before the coronavirus lockdown.

## 'Karate is about many things but first and foremost it is about training.'

Sensei F. Brennan

Sensei Frank Brennan, 8th Dan teaching white belt students before they sit their first grading.

Ashington Shotokan Karate Club students with Sensei Jill Kelly 6th Dan and Sensei Trish Bruce 6th Dan, after being selected onto the KUGB England Kata and Kumite Squads in 2020

Sensei Frank Brennan, 8th Dan teaching white belt students before they sit their first grading.

A new black belt shaking hands and receiving his licence back after successfully grading with Sensei Andy Sherry 9th Dan and Sensei Frank Brennan 8th Dan

海外に空手を広めた先生方に感謝します。
世界の空手発展に栄えあれ！

## Nippon Budokan →

The Budokan martial arts training hall, Chiyoda, Tokyo. An imposing building modelled on the octagonal Buddhist temple Yumedono (Hall of Dreams), located in Nara, Japan. Originally built as a martial arts venue for the 1964 Tokyo Olympics. On 5 August 2021, karate debuts at the Tokyo 2020 Olympic Games. Eighty of the world's best karatekas will be competing for medals in Kumite and Kata events. The ideal setting and stage for karate, the birth nation of the ancient discipline.

Photo credit: 7 September 2019 'Karate 1 Premier League'. Charly Triballeau/AFP via Getty Images

'The most important thing in the Olympic Games is not winning but taking part; the essential thing in life is not conquering but fighting well.'

Pierre de Coubertin, founder of the International Olympic Committee

The events depicted in this story took place in Norfolk and Suffolk between 2016 and 2020. At the request of the contributors, some names have been changed. Out of respect for their courage, the rest has been told exactly as it occurred.

# 'MARTIAL ARTS SAVED MY LIFE'

...just not in the way you might think.

Words: Andrew G Stewart
Pictures: Keagan Henman on Unsplash

WHY
EVERYTHING
YOU KNOW
ABOUT
MARTIAL
ARTS IS
WRONG*

43

# I have an interest in wellbeing, you know, keeping fit and healthy. Actually, I find everybody has an interest in keeping well. Don't you think?

I'm at a dinner party (I get asked occasionally) and someone asks 'What do you do to keep fit?' I say 'I do martial arts' and see the blood drain from their face.

They're thinking 'Ohhh no. Why me?' It's their one night out and they're sitting next to a martial arts fanatic – who's literally going to bore them to death. So I ask them 'What do you do, you know, to keep fit?' That usually lights them up. I then hear about their passions, a story of commitment, purpose, community and health. That shouldn't surprise you, you'll likely have

heard similar stories, it's one we sometimes share, the one about keeping upright and healthy. It's then that Fifi, the 18-year-old daughter of the host chimes in. She asks 'Could you really, like, literally kill someone?' I mean, how do I 'literally' answer that? So I do – in a heartbeat. I answer 'Yes...' And just for fun, I leave that hanging in the awkward space between my answer and the host asking 'Drink, anyone?' A more truthful reply would have been 'Yes, and so could you. If you had a bread-knife.' Conversation over, point made. But the conversation wasn't over, it was just starting. →

There's a story I like telling. It's 4 May 2016. We're at the University of East Anglia – the location of Kuk Sool Won's European Championship. I'm sitting in one of the top rows in the spectator gallery, with an impressive view of the hall, soon to be filled with hundreds of martial arts students from Europe and beyond. On my left is my training buddy, Paul Finn. Like me, he's receiving his 1st Dahn black belt today. On my right, a couple of seats away is a guy from Scotland, Calum Galbraith. He's just about to become one of only five people in Scotland to hold a 5th degree black belt in Kuk Sool Won. Turns out martial arts saved his life. But it's not what you think. He didn't defeat an angry mob in a back alley. Neither did he survive a life or death encounter in the ring. I'll get onto how he was saved in a second. First, how did Calum get here?

After training for more than 22 years, this day represents much more than just his commitment and dedication to martial arts. To be promoted to 5th Dahn Master, you've got to really want it. It takes belief to get this far. Far from where he found himself a number of years ago. Calum was at the bottom of the pile. Relationship breakdown, job tanking, spirit sinking... his only anchor, an unlikely place. His martial arts training hall – where he practised Kuk Sool Won. It was there that he found a safe harbour, with friends, also a familiar sequence that provided safety and security in a fast-changing set of spiralling circumstances. For Calum, martial arts became a life-saver. It also become a way of life. Faith keeps some people afloat. For the Scotsman, it was Kuk Sool Won that saved him.

It was the time I caught up with Claire, a teenage red belt. She trains with the adults now. There sitting on the bench, waiting for her dad to pick her up, after the training session. She'd had a better day, she met with an old school friend. Turns out Claire doesn't go to school, she's home-schooled, after a serious episode of bullying. You should see her now, sparring in the adult session – full of courage, speed and confidence, someone to contend with. Or the new student on the front row, in gym kit, unsure and apprehensive, at a first taster session. A first time, maybe a last hope. What's their story? Some people have it really rough, because bad things happen to them. But they choose to take responsibility for themselves and try to improve their circumstances. You'll likely know people like Calum, or Claire, and what these stories have in common is Kuk Sool Won, a martial art that unites the narrative and binds us together. When we train, when we commit to our craft and our community, we have an opportunity to discover things like hard circumstances, trauma and troubles. We find courage that we didn't know existed and talent despite desperate circumstances. I love the fact that people have a go – it inspires me that they invest in themselves, in the hope of a better version of today. For the red belt, it turns out she's a natural, it lights her up and she's just beginning to believe it. It's a passionate sense of potential and possibility playing out. It's the hope that we all have, just not all of the time, and that's partly what this book is all about: possibility and your potential. It's also about broadening out the conversation, providing a fuller answer to the statement: why everything you know about martial arts is wrong.

So Fifi, martial arts is less on the side of killing people, it's more about the relationship, what we might achieve and receive when it comes to martial arts. For you my reader, the training hall, gym or dojang might be a place you're familiar with. A place to overcome circumstances or discover something that otherwise might remain hidden. For others, it's an opportunity to start a journey, a new chapter, to get fitter, improve themselves, be part of something, punch and learn how to take a hit. That's the real value – and for some people, it's life-affirming and life-transforming. △

## 'It's a passionate sense of potential and possibility. It's the hope that we all have, just not all of the time.'

Calum: Kuk Sool Won gave me a safe haven, stability at a time when everything was going awry. It was the one constant that I had, one I could rely on to give me the confidence to go on. It gave me the foundations to rebuild, I stopped drinking, I got promoted at work and met a wonderful person who I married in 2018. Life is full of trials and tribulations which are set out to test our resolve. Unbeknown to me at the time, it was Kuk Sool Won that provided the structure to rebuild.

Perfection is flawless, pie in the sky, as real as a unicorn.

It might exist in the mind. But our experience, like a slap in the face, brings clarity and often an unwelcome reality. Perfection is good. Don't get me wrong. It drives us, inspires us, but it can debilitate and discourage. Pursuit of perfection, good luck with that. It's noble, for sure, but don't let perfect be the enemy of the good.

We've been conditioned to think that the right combination of actions will likely achieve the right end result. Just not all of the time. For some, experience over time tempers fleeting elation, dials down disappointment and guides the gullible.

Our experience says: 'If you can't achieve perfection, go for good instead.' After all, what's the alternative, to do nothing at all?

Maybe moderate and measure, prepare for gradual improvement, where ability and skills incrementally improve. Settle for modest momentum, satisfaction over time, where patience and commitment favour a firm foundation.

Ask what lies undiscovered, yet to be seen. That perfect kick, peachy punch or crafty combo. Maybe a terminal take down, a sensational strike or phenomenal finish?

On matters of martial arts... It might be as simple as making a start, in pursuit of perfecting the good.

**Fear, the uncomfortable bed fellow and unwelcome passenger. To fear or not to fear? That is the question.**

# FEAR NOT

What would you do if you weren't afraid?

Words: Andrew G Stewart
Pictures: Mark Ralston/AFP via Getty Images, Stephen Leonardi/Unsplash, Jimmy Chinn/National Geographic, Caleb George/Unsplash

WHY
EVERYTHING
YOU KNOW
ABOUT
MARTIAL
ARTS IS
WRONG

# What is a photograph of the 3,000-foot vertical wall of rock called El Capitan doing in a book about martial arts?

We'll get to El Capitan in a moment. First, I want you to remember a time when you faced a daunting task. It might have been a situation in life where you felt as if you were literally hanging off a rock face by your fingertips, without a safety rope. Stay with me on this. While it may be uncomfortable to recall a fearful moment, you might just discover a safety net that you never knew you had.

It might have been public speaking, a test or exam. It might have been snakes, wide-open spaces or sharp needles. Your fear might have been based on the possibility and prospect of failure, rejection, humiliation or loss. Maybe loneliness, separation or just fear of fear itself, that most primitive of emotions. Fear, the big unknown, where consequence has yet to play out – not a comfortable feeling. But whatever you fear, fear is not all bad. Fear alerts us to danger, an ancient built-in survival mechanism and it's there to keep us alive. Fear is our natural defence, triggered by memories, reinforced by experiences and our own perceptions.

You know the feeling, when threat activates alertness and grabs your attention, your pulse quickens, adrenaline spikes and your body prepares to enter combat (or drops a smoke bomb and you run like hell). Fear is complex, like a shape-shifter in the heart and the mind. We become aware of its stealth in the shadows, ready to pounce with its paralysing presence.

The sweat in our palms and maxed-out pulse, that dizzying feeling and sickly sensation. I'm curious, are you afraid of heights? Do you fear the consequences of falling, the prospect of landing at high speed? If you do, the picture on the right is not for you. That's Alex Honnold, an American rock climber. He's OK with heights; understatement of the decade. Back on the morning of 3 June 2017 just before sunrise, Alex set off with a chalk bag and a pair of climbing shoes. He went on a climb. This climb was a bit different. It was a world first. Most climbers take three to five days to climb El Capitan, Alex climbed the 2,900-foot granite monolith in 3 hours and 56 minutes. Outrageous, and not just the time. Did I mention he climbed without ropes or protection? Can you imagine that? The *New York Times* described it as 'One of the greatest athletic feats of any kind, ever.' Just the thought of what Alex did fills me with fear. Jimmy Chin, an American professional climber and photographer along with Elizabeth Chai Vasarhelyi captured the feat in an Oscar-winning documentary called *Free Solo*. It's one of the most buttock-clenching, awe-inspiring, beautiful and brilliant films you're ever likely to watch. That day in June represented a decade-long dream that became a reality, when Alex climbed El Capitan, on his own, without a rope. And here's the thing, he said that on that day he felt calm, all the way up, to the very top. So how did he manage to master his fear? →

→ Alex Honnold, Freerider route, El Capitan, Yosemite National Park © Jimmy Chin /National Geographic Image Collection

The day Alex crested El Capitan, with nothing more than a chalk bag and climbing shoes, is freakishly, spectacularly remarkable. How did Alex get to that place? How did he develop the confidence and competence to achieve such a feat and how did he conquer his fear? To explain this, we need to go back a little.

Alex Honnold has always been a climber. At the age of five he was climbing in the gym. As a teenager, he participated in national and international climbing competitions, each day exposing himself to fear. Over time, he exposed himself to bigger, more challenging climbs, inspired and encouraged by those around him. Every challenge required planning, a meticulous process and attention to detail developed over time. For Alex, as a free solo climber, without rope protection or a safety net, mistakes tend to happen just the once. Game over.

A year after his climb, Alex shared his story on the Ted talk platform. How he'd thought about the climb for around ten years, then prepared meticulously for a year and a half, committing thousands of pre-planned hand and foot moves to memory. It turns out that Alex had climbed El Capitan (with ropes) over 50 times to familiarise and practise, refine and plan in preparation for his greatest challenge. For Alex, beyond the physicality, free soloing plays out in the mind, the need to remain calm to be at your best. Alex cultivated a steely mindset by imagining and visualising the sensation of climbing and moving, committing to memory a complex sequence of pre-planned movements. So imagine you're 2,300 feet above the valley floor.

There's a ten-foot section known as the boulder problem. According to Alex, it's incredibly difficult. The hardest move on the mountain, with the worst hold on the entire route, with maybe half a thumb for purchase. To get to the next hold, it required 'karate kicking' one leg to reach a toehold, a move that required a high degree of flexibility and accuracy. One that Alex practised and rehearsed more than 60 times, then (thankfully) executed with perfect precision. To watch this moment was terrifying, simultaneously the best and worst part of the documentary.

Alex also considered not just the physicality of the challenge, he thought about the emotional component. What if he got up there and it was too scary? How about if he got too tired or froze with fear? What if he remained on the ground, too fearful to try? How would he live with that? It's hard to wrap words around an answer – It's what sets Alex Honnold apart, where he's taken preparation to new extremes and appears able to simply turn off his body's fear response. There is a suggestion that repeated exposure to fears might lead to familiarity, which in turn can reduce the fear response. For Alex, he feels most alive on the challenge, the unknown and discovery of limits – the feeling of setting goals and self-improvement. His mantra 'Doubt is the precursor to fear. Visualise and rehearse until doubt becomes so diminished, that you know what you need to do – the problem or challenge that you hope to overcome.' On that day in June, Alex had no doubts, he had perfectly executed his routine in his mind and without hesitation, he achieved mastery that day in 3 hours 56 minutes. →

← THE BOULDER PROBLEM 2,300 FEET ABOVE THE VALLEY FLOOR

'Doubt is the precursor to fear. Visualise and rehearse until doubt becomes so diminished, that you know what you need to do – the problem or challenge that you hope to overcome.'

Alex Honnold, Rock Climber

In life, everything has a spectrum of risk and consequence, reward and recognition. Frequency of the everyday habituates us to risks like driving a car or just leaving the house. For some, fear stands for Forget Everything And Run, or Face Everything And Rise. To face a particular fear is a suggestion that we have an opportunity to do something that might just diminish fear's power and enable us to achieve things we never though possible. A first step might start with acknowledging and accepting fear's presence. To then unlock and unravel the fearful might mean digging in the hope of unearthing the reasons. To then ask and hopefully answer the 'What if...?' questions, then develop a plan to build competence and confidence that might buttress our belief then counter the boulders of fear and doubt. That might mean you need to do something new, something different and courageous. For me, it was saying 'yes' to the question 'Will you be my best man?', taking on the responsibility for officiating at my cousin Al's wedding in Helsinki and delivering a eulogy at my sister-in-law's funeral. It was also saying 'yes' to a martial arts taster session with my six-year-old son Loui, a little over ten years ago.

There's a climbing route on El Capitan called Lurking Fear which captures the thrust of this narrative well. While fear is an uncomfortable bedfellow, an unwelcome passenger, it is always present. Alex mastered his fear and achieved his ambition. How about you? What is your mountain, your El Capitan? △

← Freerider route, El Capitan,
Yosemite National Park
© Caleb George / Unsplash

Situations can tip over into chaos in a heartbeat, in a million different ways. Violence is an expression of outrage and frustration, an impulse that crushes rational thinking and reason. An in-built aggression, ready to ignite the fight under the banners of dominance and malice, disrespect and retribution.

Ask yourself, what stops violence from threatening boundaries? What tactics can prevent violence from riding over accepted behavioural norms and slam into chaos at full speed?

It might be co-operation or fear of consequence, even the prospect of loss. Maybe the need to offend less easily and let go of our ego. To restrain ourselves, retrain our implanted human nature. Temper our triggers, reflect on 'The Better Angels of Our Nature',[8] where empathy, self-control, compassion and forgiveness have a chance to counter the consequence and causes of chaos.

Martial arts deploy training with the aim of dialling down escalation, thus diminishing the prospect of spiralling violence. So are there ever conditions that validate violence? Under certain conditions and circumstances, to fight back in the face of adversity, to counter the violent actions of others. In a curated fight, competition or sport, violence happens with consent under agreed rules, rather than arising out of hatred or vengeful retribution.

To foster an alternative perspective, a different vantage point designed to diminish anger and vengefulness. 'When they go low, we go high.'[8] Michelle Obama's motto for exercising restraint under fire. Perhaps turn the other cheek,[10] a response that's less about being meek or weak, more about defiance than worldly compliance.

'Violence, after all, is no mystery. It's peace that's the mystery. Violence is the default. It's easy. It's peace that is difficult: learned, inculcated, earned.'

Jordan B. Peterson, 12 Rules for Life: An Antidote to Chaos

The Ultimate Fighting Championship (UFC) is an American mixed martial arts (MMA) promotion company based in Las Vegas. In 2016, UFC sold for an eye-watering $4 billion.

# FIGHT CLUB

What's behind the billionaire business of brawling?

Words: Andrew G Stewart
Pictures: Shutterstock; Christian Petersen/Getty Images; Pablo Rebolledo/Unsplash

WHY
EVERYTHING
YOU KNOW
ABOUT
MARTIAL
ARTS IS
WRONG*

UFC is a modern phenomenon, a highly curated fight experience, where at a safe distance, we witness the ancient warrior spirit and creed. While MMA is not for everyone, at times brutal cage fighting, it is rooted in the realities of combat.

## UFC 189 / 12 Jul 2015

Venue: MGM Grand Garden Arena.

Two title fights headlined that night. The top billing, an ultimate grudge match between UFC featherweight champion Jose Aldo and challenger 'The Notorious' Conor McGregor. Jose Aldo dropped out with injury, in steps Chad Mendes. McGregor overcame Mendes, at the end of Round 2. But it was the welterweight undercard fight between Rory MacDonald and Robbie Lawler that stole the show. Brutal, intense, ferocious, unforgiving. It's what happens when two fighters at the top of their game choose not to back down.

# The fight is the opposite of order, balance and calm. It's the underworld. It's ancient, hard-wired primeval survival that's unscripted, unwritten and sometimes unavoidable.

Ever since there has been a reason to fight, it's caused a spectacle. A mammoth rib pinched from a Stone Age camp fire, a grudge match headlining at the Colosseum or a misunderstanding outside the high-street kebab shop. All of us at some point have either witnessed or been part of a fight. Whether participating wilfully or reluctantly, a bystander baying for blood or a passing pedestrian, there can be few other such experiences in life that bring out the worst in people. Also, curiously, the best in people. Take the professional fighter, when viewed through the lens of the paid-up spectator. It can be hard to tear yourself away from the drama unfolding – there's something magnetic about the contest. Will the big guy prevail, what's the angle, forget the reason. Fight's on.

Fighting is a natural consequence of living. Evolution and survival, biology and being, cause and effect. To fight for your rights, protect and defend status or command respect. Thankfully, according to the acclaimed author Steven Pinker, in his book *The Better Angels of Our Nature*, world violence has declined considerably over time. The story inside the ring, however, 'the fight' is as popular as ever, drawing the crowds from small circles to mammoth gatherings. The 'Rumble in the Jungle', when Ali met George Foreman in Zaire, or 'The Thrilla in Manila' when Ali defended his heavyweight title against his greatest rival, Joe Frazier (pictured). The roll call of all time greats: Jack Johnson, Muhammad Ali, Sugar Ray Robinson, Manny Pacquiao, Rocky Marciano, George Foreman, Lennox Lewis, Julio Cesar Chavez. Impossible to leave out Tyson, both Fury and Iron Mike. Also impossible to mention all the greats – but each fighter, each contest drew millions of people and millions by way of financial returns. So what of the billionaire business of modern-day brawling? When did Mixed Martial Arts go mainstream and what is UFC all about? To explain this, first, we have to go back in time, to the 33rd Olympics, 648 BC. Back then, you might have been a spectator watching Kallias of Athens locked in combat with Dorieus of Rhodes. The form of combat: Pankration, a deadly martial art from ancient Greece. A combination of wrestling and boxing, where almost anything goes. Its name derives from the ancient Greek words *pan* (all) and *kratos* (strength, might and power) and literally means 'all force'. Back then, the Greeks regarded Pankration as the ultimate test in strength and technique. So what's changed? →

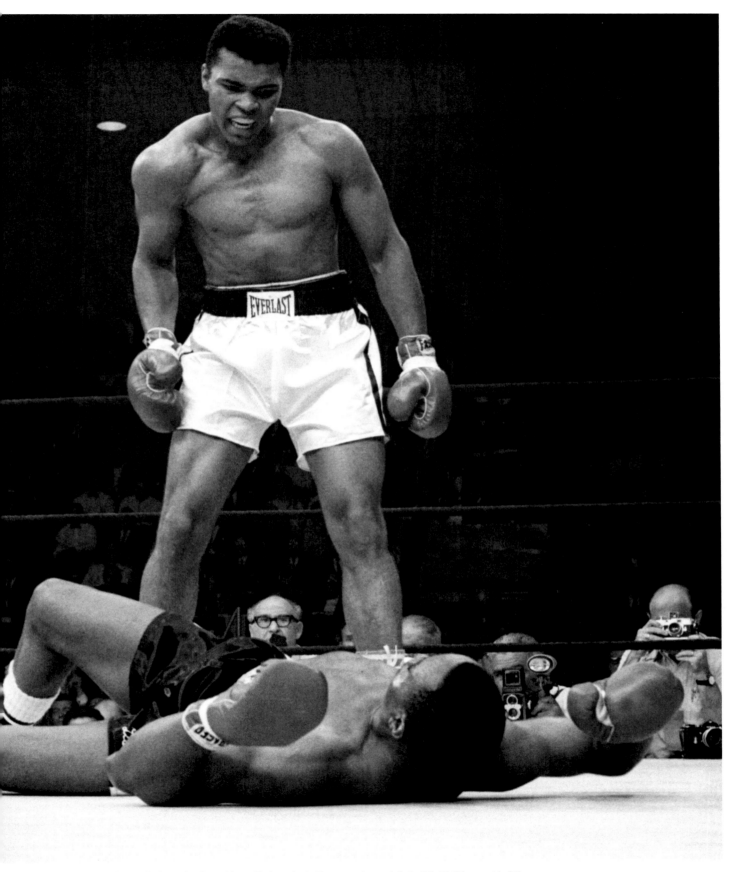

↑ 25 May 1965. Muhammad Ali taunting Sonny Liston (2nd meeting). Ali won, controversially, by KO at 2:12 in round 1 of 15.
Credit: Bettmann/Getty images.

Fast forward to the late twentieth century, November 1993, The Ultimate Fighting Championship (UFC) is born. An organization based in Las Vegas, Nevada which revolutionized Mixed Martial Arts competition. To be clear, MMA is the sport, UFC is the major organisation and promoter within the sport of MMA. The UFC's ambition, to find the ultimate fighting champion – sounds very Hollywood. But this is for real, like a street fight featuring the best athletes in the world skilled in karate, jiu-jitsu, boxing, kickboxing, grappling, wrestling, sumo and other combat sports. UFC was originally set up by Rorion Gracie, grandmaster of jiu-jitsu, and three partners. One was John Milius, who wrote and directed *Conan the Barbarian* back in 1982, the others Art Davie, an advertising executive and Bob Meyrowitz, a pioneer of pay-per-view TV. Over time UFC has transformed the art of fighting, exploding onto the global market. Now broadcasting to over 165 countries, a billion households worldwide in 40 different languages, on-demand fighting is now the premier destination for fight fans and fighters alike.

In 2016 UFC broke more than just the odd nose, breaking new ground with a world-leading UFC Performance Institute, focused on 'delivering the world's best MMA training facilities to support the scientific development of athletes and coaches, injury prevention, recovery, treatment and rehabilitation of professional athletes.' That same year, the UFC changed hands for close to a staggering $4 billion to a group led by Hollywood talent agency WME-IMG.

What's clear is that we're now living in an era of the celebrity fighter, where the likes of professional mixed martial artist Conor McGregor, nicknamed 'The Notorious' has dominated the fight channels since his 2013 UFC debut. With an estimated net worth of £100m, according to Forbes, his crossover boxing match against Floyd Mayweather in 2017 and sponsorships deals all adding to his fortune both in and outside the UFC Octagon. Take a closer look at the picture on the right, Robbie Lawler, the fighter facing you. His tattoos, do you recognise the tattoo on his left arm? It depicts the Colosseum and the gladiator – it's what they are. Modern-day gladiators. A spectacular list of UFC Hall of Famers including Bas Rutten, Randy Couture, Georges St-Pierre, Tito Ortiz and Ken Shamrock. More recently, Anderson Silva, WWE star Brock Lesnar, Khabib Nurmagomedov, Michael Bisping, BJ Penn, Robbie Lawler and welterweight fighter Rory Macdonald and of course 'The Notorious' Conor McGregor. As for the female fighters, Cris Cyborg, Joanna Jedrzejczyk, Amanda Nunes and Rose Namajunas to name a few – all kings and queens of the cage.

There is no denying the fighter's skill, great stamina and heart. Whether over in seconds or a full five rounds of gore, a thumbs up or a thumbs down, the public are paying like never before. To the spectator, UFC demonstrates and showcases a multitude of hybrid styles, high-stakes, visceral violence and rivalry, where lives and livelihoods, not to mention reputations, play out in real time. UFC is a modern phenomenon, a highly curated fight experience, where at a safe distance, we witness the ancient warrior spirit and creed. While MMA is not for everyone, at times brutal cage fighting, it is rooted in the realities of combat. An end-game which remains unchanged and brutally simple, the fighter's ambition, to wrestle, strike or grapple their opponent to submission, stoppage, TKO or KO.

As for the future of MMA, UFC President Dana White has plans. He's quoted as saying 'I'm gonna blow you away with what we're going to do'. Somehow I don't think he's kidding. In an article in the *Guardian*, back in 2016, in the words of one of the Fertitta brothers who sold UFC to WME-IMG 'What we have is this incredible thing where you take two athletes, at the top of their game, in the most incredible shape and you put them in the Octagon and you let them use any martial art they want to compete. And it translates. Immediately. Overnight.' 'No matter what colour you are, what language you speak, what country you are from. It is fighting. And at some level, people get it.' △

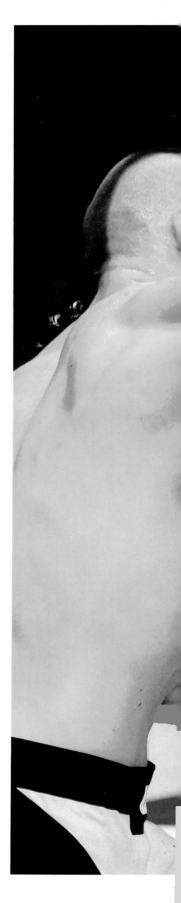

## 'You put the Devil on the other side, and I will come to fight.'

Royce Gracie, Brazilian Mixed Martial Artist

↑ UFC 189 / 12 July 2015, Robbie Lawler (right) and former UFC welterweight fighter/title contender Rory Macdonald. Brutal, intense, ferocious, unforgiving. Credit: Josh Hedges/Getty images.

**WHY
EVERYTHING
YOU KNOW
ABOUT
MARTIAL
ARTS IS
WRONG***

↑ Left to right:
PKJN John Garrod, 5TH Dahn Master
JIKJN Paul Taylor, 6TH Dahn Master
SU SUHK KJN Sunjin, 9TH Dahn Master
SU HN IM KJN John Ives, 8TH Dahn Master
JIKJN Nick Reeve, 6TH Dahn Master

↑ Left to right:
JIKJN Paul Taylor, 6TH Dahn Master
SBN Leanne Taylor, 4TH Dahn Master
SU SUHK KJN Sunjin, 9TH Dahn Master
PKJN John Garrod, 5TH Dahn Master

# What question would you ask?

# INTERVIEW WITH THE MASTERS

↑ Left to right: PKJN John Garrod, 5ᵀᴴ Dahn Master
JIKJN Paul Taylor, 6ᵀᴴ Dahn Master

**Participants:** John Garrod, 5ᵀᴴ Dahn Master, Kuk Sool Won; Paul Taylor, 6ᵀᴴ Dahn Master, Kuk Sool Won.
**Interviewer:** Andrew G Stewart, 1ˢᵀ Dahn, Kuk Sool Won.
**Date & Location:** 12 May 2020, via Zoom (online) during the Corona Virus Pandemic lockdown.
**Pictures:** Used with kind permission of Marcus Horsley-Rai, 2ᴺᴰ Dahn Kuk Sool Won; Gavin E. Churcher.

I've just collected Loui from primary school. He's six, I'm a little over 36 and as I unpack his Lightning McQueen school bag, crumpled at the bottom is a piece of paper. When un-crumpled, it reads 'Kuk Sool Won Martial Arts – Free Taster Session'. It's taking place at a local sports hall, and I think 'I've not heard of that one "Kuk Sool Won", might give it go.' I used to do Shotokan Karate, a million years ago. Kuk Sool Won might work for Loui, help develop his confidence, maybe build resilience. So we arrive at the sports hall, not sure what to expect. That's when I first met John Garrod and Paul Taylor. Dressed in their finery, their martial art outfits. Super-friendly and approachable, with an air of steeliness and calm self-assurance.

Time is slippery stuff, that was back in the summer of 2009. Fast-forward to now, spring 2020. John and Paul run successful martial arts schools in the East of England, Ipswich and Woodbridge respectively. For John and Paul, martial arts runs deep, martial arts *is* family, literally. Paul is John's son-in-law, he married John's daughter Leanne (currently testing to become a 5TH Dahn Master) after they met at the World Kuk Sool Won Championships in Korea, back in 2005.

Since that first taste and see session, we've trained together for over a decade. I'm proud to say that John and Paul are my masters. Over the years, they have taught and inspired me and countless others to reach levels of martial art competence I never though possible. It's also been great fun, to be part of a community, contribute to training and feel part of something. Something that this interview hopes to unpack and share with you.

John: It's always been up to the student, to determine their level of commitment. To ask the question 'What's important to me?' Then line themselves up behind the answer, maybe take a step and make a commitment. When they do that, that's when change happens, that's what I really love to see.

So what makes a good interview? Maybe unearthing a truth you otherwise wouldn't be aware of, perhaps something that changes your world view or helps you down the track. I think co-operation, trust and participation are factors, asking the right questions, that's a good place to start. As interviewer, boredom is failure. I'll try to avoid that one. My goal: to curate something that might surprise you, maybe inspire you and put you, as reader, right into the conversation. Into the empty chair beside us.

**Andy:** OK, we'll start with the easy questions. Who's your favourite martial arts hero and why?

John: Bruce Lee, he was the one who got me into martial arts. The movie, *Way of the Dragon*, with Chuck Norris. Bruce Lee takes his fighting style to another level.

Paul: My mum said when I was younger, I'd watch Bruce Lee all the time on VHS. Back in 1984, Jean-Claude Van Damme, he was my hero. I watched *Kick Boxer* just last night, what a legend. Mum said I would dress like JCVD, in a tight suit, like the one he wore in AWOL. I was ten mind!

**Andy:** You've been doing martial arts for ever. What got you both started?

Paul: Getting bullied. Aged nine, I wasn't stocky back then. I was picked on and my parents had a word with my uncle. He knew Steve Isaacson, he ran a Kuk Sool Won school in Mildenhall, Suffolk. After a taster session, Steve took me under his wing and to this day he's remained a close friend and mentor. He's now a 7TH Dahn Master.

John: After seeing the movies I guess, martial arts fascinated me. I wanted to look after myself, learn self-defence more than anything. At 21, I went to the local YMCA, met Mick Blackwell, also Billy Brennan, both highly regarded in the world of martial arts. I did karate for around six years, helping out, and the people were great. Met with Karate legend Ticky Donovan, now 9TH Dahn I think. I then damaged my cruciate ligament playing football, so I stepped back from sport for a while. Kuk Sool Won came later, a few years later, I was 41 when I started Kuk Sool Won.

**Andy:** Why Kuk Sool Won and not Kung Fu, Karate or Taekwondo?

**John:** Karate was great, but after a while, I was looking for something different. When my daughters Leanne and Rachel came home from school, they had a slip of paper in their bags – a 'Taste and See'. A demo at a local school. When I turned up, I saw a room full of people with black uniforms with Kuk Sool Won on the back. I remember thinking 'What the hell is this?' It was packed, the kicks were similar to what I'd learnt in karate. Then the self-defence techniques were demonstrated, and I thought WOW, I like the look of that. I met Martin Ducker that night, then spoke with him about my injury and he said come along, give it a try, we can work around your injury. I never looked back. That was in 1984. I remember being asked by Martin what my ambition was, my answer, to run a martial art school. I'm now close friends with Martin and his wife Alison, they run a great school based in Lowestoft and Halesworth [in Suffolk].

**Paul:** My uncle, he introduced me to the only martial art club near me, Kuk Sool Won, which originally started on the airbase at Mildenhall. It was local, that's when I met Steve Isaacson. Kuk Sool Won is different from so many other martial arts which can be a bit samey samey, kicking and punching. If that works for you, great. In Kuk Sool Won, there is so much to learn, as a martial arts system, Kuk Sool Won covers loads of aspects beyond just kicking and punching, like break falling, joint locks, breathing and meditation techniques.

**Andy:** That's fascinating. Some people may not be aware of the depth or variety in Kuk Sool Won. I have to ask, have you ever found yourself cornered, where your martial arts skills saved your life?

**John:** No. Maybe a confrontation at a bar, nothing came of it though. I've been lucky, I've not had to use it.

**Paul:** Hmmm, De Niro's nightclub, Newmarket. I was in my early 20s. There was a woman involved, isn't there always! Her boyfriend wasn't happy. Martial arts has taught me that sometimes the best thing to do is walk away. That night, I found myself at the top of the stairs, on my way out. I'd also heard he had a knife. As he approached, knife partially concealed in his hand, coming up the stairs towards me, I had no chance of exit. Next thing, he's at the bottom of the stairs, a bit dazed! It happened so fast. For me, to look after my family is massive, to check out surroundings, exits, security. Not always, but to look out for people, make sure the people I'm with are safe.

**Andy:** Do you have a favourite signature move?

**John:** Run! (We all have a laugh at that one). Context is important. In the real world, I think that's not a bad starting point.

**Paul:** Confront the situation, use your head. If you can, walk away. Protect your family and friends.

**Andy:** OK, so let me change the question, the context. It's tournament time, you've got a window for your perfect move, the one you've practised, maybe one of Jean-Claude Van Damme's moves – so what's it going be?

**John:** Draw them in with a few low front snap kicks, then on the third or fourth, fake front snap kick, pivot, then land a high roundhouse. Worked for me back then.

**Paul:** Spinning crescent kick, back in the day, for demo. Spinning back fist, if they're not too big, in tournaments, maybe basic back fist.

**Andy:** Nice, I'll remember that when we next go toe to toe Paul. So now your children and grandchildren train, why is that important to you?

**John:** It wasn't. They wanted to do it, it was their choice and it built their confidence. Daniel got to 1ST Dahn, Rachel got to 2ND Dahn and Leanne is now testing for her 5TH Dahn Masters, the grandkids are now training, which is great to see. For me, it's not so much about the perfect kick or punch, it not even about medals and certificates, which are important, don't get me wrong. I think it's more about self-respect and building confidence.

**Paul:** My kids Chloe and Liam trained for years. Now Evie and Bobby love training. →

Paul: When people walk through the door, their first thoughts, when it comes to martial arts is often MMA [Mixed Martial Arts]. All they think about is the octagon cage, gloves on where fighters kick the sh*t out of each other. That's what we're up against.

↑ JIKJN Paul Taylor, 6ᵀᴴ Dahn Master. Form demonstration. KSW European Championships, UEA: University of East Anglia, Norwich.

For me, to go to work and know that my kids can defend themselves – that's really important. As long as they aren't the instigator, they need to feel they can defend themselves. They make me proud, all of them, to see them training and developing. It's like when parents of students tell me that their kids are taking responsibility for themselves, they can see the changes. That's great. For parents of kids doing martial arts, its also about taking what they learn for an hour a week and applying at home. Things like respect and discipline, that's when they see the changes. Not every time though.

**Andy:** **If you could see a change in what people think about martial arts, what would that be?**

**John:** It's not just about kicking and punching. If people could catch that. It's about discipline, respect, building confidence and growth. To teach kids to learn to stand up for themselves, be prepared and ready for a situation. If they can learn to kick and punch, don't get me wrong, that's a bonus.

**Paul:** When people walk through the door, their first thoughts, when it comes to martial arts is often MMA [Mixed Martial Arts]. All they think about is the octagon cage, gloves on where fighters kick the sh*t out of each other. That's what we're up against. When our students are in their sparring kit, wearing protection, it's non-contact. They wear the gear just in case, because accidents can happen. Some say they want their boy to fight professionally, MMA, like Conor McGregor. They don't understand just how hard it is to be a professional fighter. It's very different from the Kuk Sool Won martial art syllabus. It's not like catching bullets in your teeth, but movies play a part – actors like the mixed martial art actor Scott Adkins might get people interested in martial arts, and that has to be a good thing. His martial arts are amazing, he's a black belt in loads of styles, Taekwondo, kickboxing, Karate, jiu-jitsu and Kung Fu I think.

**John:** That's right, it goes way beyond just kicking and punching, where students have the chance to develop over time. It can take years to really get to grips with some of the techniques, weapons and forms.

**Paul:** It does take time, you get to 1ST Dahn, and that's just the start. Even at 5TH Dahn Master, there is so much to learn, it's a continuous journey. It's also about adapting, take John, he's just had a hip replacement, I wouldn't expect him to be running up the wall doing a jumping roundhouse. Mind, if he didn't, he'd have to do 1,000 push-ups [we all have a laugh at that one].

**Andy:** **When you look back, what has martial arts given you?**

**John:** A different attitude towards life. Generally, the way you look at things. In a way, more rational, you know what I mean? Calmer. I know at times it's hard, life, at work, something might happen, you have to evaluate more rationally. You might snap, say 'for f*ck sake' when you get an awkward customer. You learn to take a step back, respect the individual and the situation. That and a stronger mind, more resilient, clearer in a way, you learn to see the positive.

**Paul:** John's nailed it. That's it. Everything John's just said. You develop respect and self-control, most of the time, I'm not perfect! Kuk Sool Won has given me so much over the years, I met my wife Leanne (John's daughter), we've had two lovely kids together. Kuk Sool Won is my family.

**John:** Same with me, I met Martin and his wife Alison. If I had a problem, they would do anything for us, it's great. Friendship, community, we're all on a shared journey.

**Paul:** In my 37 years of training and John's 25, the number of friends we've made, the people we've met. Take Steve Isaacson, he was the best man at my wedding.

**John:** That's the other thing, commitment. Some people think it's instant, a quick fix. It isn't. It takes time.

**Andy:** **What for you makes the last 25+ years of dedication worth all the time, commitment and patience?**

**John:** Personally, getting my 5TH Dahn Masters. Also seeing students progress and change in a good way, you know. →

The friendships, also where a nervous student, like Katherine, who is now a brown belt. She spent time researching different martial arts and settled on Kuk Sool Won. She has done amazingly well, so much more confident and a superb student. Or Jen, the confidence she's gained, after being bullied at school. You're doing something for another person, you're giving back.

**Paul:** Same thing really. My 1ˢᵀ Dahn, and now my 6ᵀᴴ Dahn, after 12 years training as a Master. When students enter my dojang and return week after week. The diabetic student who has lost weight, grown in confidence, built friendships. We've had our stories, I'm not at the end of mine, but you know what I mean. We can speak into Evie's story, Bobby's story our students stories. Also, when I met the Grandmaster In Hyuk Suh back in '89. Back then, when you grabbed his wrist, you knew about it. When we used to do seminars, he would put you on your arse, he was phenomenal. He knocked me out, and Steve Isaacson, twice in 10 minutes! He was just that good. To this day, he stands alone, he knows his stuff. He might be in his early 80s but he will always remain a legend.

**Andy:** In so many ways, what a privilege to have met In Hyuk Suh, the author, creator, perfecter and founder of this martial art. It's unique, the way he talks about Kuk Sool Won not so much as a sport or style, much more a system. You only get to know and appreciate that when you train.

**Andy:** On to achievements, and I know you guys are a bit on the humble side, what's in the trophy cabinet?

**John:** We've both been Grand Champions. Paul was European Grand Champion back in 96/97. I was Grand Champion maybe three times, as 2ᴺᴰ Dahn, in the over 40s category. I can't remember the years to be honest. But I'll never lose sight of what it feels like, to see new joiners start nervously, then build in confidence and win a medal at the European Championships. That's great. To be honest, it's not just about the medals, and it's not even all about the belts and certificates. You see first-hand how students start to grow in confidence, develop physically and emotionally. How they start to believe in themselves, execute a technique under pressure. The smile on their faces when they do it, the look on their parent's faces, that makes it worth it. You don't take that for granted, you don't forget that.

**Andy:** John and Paul... What can I say, thanks so much. I really appreciate your insights and honesty. It's safe to say that when people read this, they'll get that martial arts is about more than just catching bullets in your teeth.

Truth is, I don't know how many photocopied fliers were given out that day at school, back in 2009. Many likely remained in bags, never to be opened. I sometimes wonder 'What if Loui had come home with a ballroom dancing taste and see leaflet?' Ten years on, I might be a black belt dancer, and you might be reading a book on ballroom dancing! But he didn't. It was Kuk Sool Won. Turns out it was always going to be Kuk Sool Won. △

John: You see first-hand how students start to grow in confidence, develop physically and emotionally. How they start to believe in themselves, execute a technique under pressure. The smile on their faces when they do it, the look on their parent's faces, that makes it worth it. You don't take that for granted, you don't forget that.

↑ PKJN John Garrod, 5ᵀᴴ Dahn Master. A keen eye for detail. KSW European Championships, UEA: University of East Anglia, Norwich.

'Kuk' refers to Nation State or Country. 'Sool' means martial art technique, but the implied meaning goes way deeper than techniques. It includes the mental, spiritual, cultural and philosophical heritage of Korean Martial Arts. 'Won' means institution or association.

# KUK SOOL WHAT?

'Kuk Sool Won', I remember repeating,
'It's a traditional Korean martial art.'

→ Founder, Grandmaster and President of the World Kuk Sool Association, In Hyuk Suh congratulating a newly promoted student. A moment to be cherished, never forgotten.

Words: Andrew G Stewart
Pictures: Marcus Horsley-Rai and Gavin E. Churcher

# Kuk Sool Won™ integrates the spectrum of established Asian martial arts and unifies them under one coherent and comprehensive system. Kuk Sool Won is also about growth, personal development and perhaps surprisingly, family.

Loui, my six-year-old son and I had just attended our first taster session at Kuk Sool Won, Ipswich, the county town of Suffolk. I was on my mobile phone speaking to my mum, Loui's Grannie, when she said 'Kuk Sool What?' I remember repeating, 'Kuk Sool Won mum, it's a traditional Korean martial art, developed in the late 1950s.' The name wasn't familiar to my mother. Ten years on, we both still refer to it as martial arts, it's easier that way. But what is Kuk Sool Won? To answer that question, I'll need to go back a little.

In the mid-1950s, in Kowloon, Hong Kong, a teenager was being taught a traditional Southern Chinese form of Kung Fu by the renowned Wing Chun master, Yip Man. You'll likely have heard of the student, Bruce Lee, a name synonymous with Kung Fu and the world of martial arts. When it comes to martial arts, we tend to think 'Karate Kid' or Judo, Olympic Taekwondo and perhaps more recently, UFC and mixed martial arts. If you're familiar with martial arts, you might also have heard of Muay Thai, Brazilian jiu-jitsu, Aikido and maybe even Krav Maga, a military self-defence and fighting

system developed for the Israeli Defence Force. Each can be described as a martial art, a codified system that in many cases embodies cultural and traditional forms of self-defence and combat.

At about the same time the teenage Bruce Lee was learning Wing Chun, a young In Hyuk Suh was visiting hundreds of martial art masters in villages and temples all over Korea.[11] In Hyuk Suh studied many aspects of traditional Korean martial arts from three major traditions: tribal martial arts, Buddhist martial arts and royal court martial arts. After many years of dedicated study, In Hyuk Suh founded Kuk Sool Won in 1958. As Grandmaster and President of the World Kuk Sool Association, In Hyuk Suh describes the martial art as a traditional Korean martial art which integrates the spectrum of established Asian fighting arts, unified under one coherent system.[12] Kuk Sool Won has grown exponentially since those early days in Korea. Sixty years on, the World Kuk Sool Association, now based in Houston, Texas, has over 1.3 million members, over 800 schools in 27 different countries.[13] →

Described as a systematic study of all the traditional Asian fighting arts, Kuk Sool Won forms a living legacy, a continuation of Korea's rich martial art heritage. As a comprehensive martial art system, Kuk Sool Won a covers a broad spectrum of techniques, training and instruction, drawn deeply from Korea's rich traditions. The syllabus includes arm and leg techniques, grappling, throws, joint locks, acrobatics and agility techniques, body conditioning, acupressure, pressure points, traditional weapons as well as meditation and breathing techniques – quite a list! Teaching and training focuses on self-defence, discipline and respect, with forms (a sequence of defined moves), techniques and sparring providing a foundation designed to temper our bodies, refine our minds and build resilience. As with many Asian martial arts, one of the principle ambitions is to 'perfect the self'[14] to consider and nurture the union, harmony and relationship between the physical aesthetic, as well as our mental and spiritual selves. It follows that teaching and training centres on self-improvement, discipline, etiquette, resilience, health and wellbeing, both physical and mental development, where repetition of movements and techniques aim to refine and develop practitioners of all ages and abilities over time. As in life, when it comes to participating in martial arts, we're wired to connect with each other. To be part of community, something so much bigger than just ourselves, and while not exclusive, Kuk Sool Won provides one such community. A safe environment where people of all ages and abilities have an opportunity to learn together, explore limits and have fun. Kuk Sool Won is local and national, practised all over the world. Like one big family, we share

both the language and culture of a traditional Korean martial art. Like a universal language, Kuk Sool Won unites us across borders and cultures, a shared ethos and spirit, where the value is realised through participation. Training often goes way beyond the curriculum, where we discover a place where relationships develop, bonds are forged and friendships thrive – it's a martial art family thing. In the words of author J.B. McGee 'I've learned through the years that it's not where you live, it's the people who surround you that make you feel at home.' It's Calum's story, captured in the feature 'Martial Arts Saved My Life' on page 42, it's Jen's story and it might also be a story that you share.

After that first taster session, Loui and I had a choice, 'Do we go back or not?' Behind that first question lay many others like 'What's the commitment?', 'Did we connect with the ethos, spirit and personality of the teachers?', 'Will I look cool in the outfit?' [I didn't mean that] and 'What's the cost?' To not forget that you're paying for a service, the question then becomes 'What do we actually receive?' Yes, we pay for instruction and expertise, tuition centred on improving competencies when it comes to matters of self-defence and combat. Having said that, Kuk Sool Won also nurtures personal development through which we hope to gain a sense of agency and self-confidence. Yes, it's a place to manage and maintain levels of fitness and flexibility as well as hone and improve levels of martial art skills and competency, but the benefits, I believe, also go way beyond our individual gains. They extend to others, where we have an opportunity to give as well as receive. That's relational, the power of giving, supporting, helping and contributing to one another. →

# 'I've learned through the years that it's not where you live, it's the people who surround you that make you feel at home.'

J.B. McGee, Author

As a practising martial artist, the rhythm, repetition and order of Kuk Sool Won fits my character. So does the balance between sparring, forms, techniques and weapons training. That combat, in particular sparring, is less MMA submission, more on the side of point sparring, not so much full contact cage fighting. That's the context of sparring in Kuk Sool Won, and that's important. Light contact, or in some cases no contact, which might sound weird. Stay with me on this. When light touch sparring, if you get through the guard, it's more on the side of control to *not* go for the knock out. Although it's a live scenario, people can and do get hit from time to time – hence the rules that govern the engagement as well as protective equipment like gloves, pads, head gear and mouth-guard. For me, with a boxing background, to also factor distance, timing, range, angles, tempo and rhythm have proved useful, an opportunity to light people up at close range.

When it comes to any form of sparring competition, it's not straightforward. Ramsey Dewey, a very experienced MMA coach and ex-professional fighter sums it up well when he states 'One of the most difficult parts of all martial arts competition is not just getting experience with fighting, it's getting in front of the crowd, in front of people, experiencing performance anxiety.' If you put on the gloves, there are stakes, you win some, you lose some, there is a lot to gain from that experience. When it comes to Kuk Sool Won, touch point sparring, light and no contact is the context. Taking care of your partner is part of the deal, to go light and learn from one another, not deliberately hurt each other. Where there is equity in the form of combat – you both abide by the same rules, the same martial art, the only difference being competence, skill, experience and application of the practitioner. Context, the circumstances that form the setting. It's why the phrase 'It's like bringing a knife to a gunfight' works so well. Sure, a knife is a deadly weapon, but a person with a gun has an inherent advantage. Illustrated perfectly by Indiana Jones in *Raiders of the Lost Ark*. The crowd in a busy Cairo marketplace suddenly parts as a black-robed swordsman confronts Jones with an over-sized scimitar. With a world-weary expression, Jones pulls out his pistol. The outcome is inevitable. So is Kuk Sool Won good for the streets? Ramsey's answer pretty much nails it 'Nothing's good for the streets. Don't get into street fights. Now get out there and train'.

To the casual observer, there are times when martial arts can appear theatrical, where a compliant opponent plays along with a scripted narrative. And that's part of it, where practitioners together demonstrate techniques, weapons and pressure points on one another. To remember that the practitioner does not wish to mortally would or disable their compliant assistant. It gets interesting when you mix that up. Literally, mixed martial arts showcases any number of styles and that's part of the allure. Which style is best, most effective and victorious in combat? That of course is dependent on any number of factors including genetics, training, competency, fitness, aggression, stamina and courage of the combatant. To not also forget the role of sheer dumb luck, when a guard is dropped at the point a strike is inbound. It's part of the reason UFC (Ultimate Fighting Championship) has been so successful – it's the street fight playing out in real time in the Octagon. You can read more about that in the feature Fight Club on page 60. ➔

## 'Learning how to fight without sparring is like learning how to swim on dry land.'

Bruce Lee

In the interview on page 68, 5<sup>TH</sup> Dahn Master John Garrod and 6<sup>TH</sup> Dahn Master Paul Taylor remind us of the dedication and commitment associated with running successful martial art schools in the UK. While 2020 has been a year of lockdown and loss for so many, it's also a year that represents a milestone for martial art school owner and founder John Garrod. It marks the 25th anniversary of his martial arts school. A quarter-century of moments and experiences, the provision of a place and a space for countless people over the years, from all walks of life, where they have benefited from the breadth and depth of learning and taking part in the art of Kuk Sool Won. Students have had the opportunity to test and try out, demonstrate their competencies. When they do, it's as if those present reflect back a different version of who they are, and perhaps for the first time, they start to believe a new story about themselves. A chunk of self-doubt dissolves, replaced by an increase in self-esteem and belief. And here's the thing, for the most part, the real benefit is what people learn in the dojang or the training hall and apply to every day life. That's not exclusive to Ipswich or Woodbridge schools, even Kuk Sool Won. It's something that can be discovered and experienced in so many martial art schools all over the world. To also witness the tireless commitment of martial art school owners and a legion of volunteers who invest their time and passion in support of helping others discover a sense of agency. Talents that may otherwise remain hidden, and not just skills associated with self-defence, combat, medals and titles. It's where people have an opportunity to discover themes of family, friendship and community. Places that encourage people to go further and dig deeper in search of improving competency and confidence, maybe find a sense of value, purpose and significance in the place they find themselves. This feature and this book is an attempt to unpack the 'why?' behind martial arts, where a collection of carefully curated stories and accounts attempt to present what we might receive when we choose to take part. Some stories may inspire and enlighten, others may appear just plain weird. But together they attempt to share the broader narrative, captured under the rather presumptuous title *Why Everything You Know About Martial Arts Is Wrong*. Granted, the unicorn piece on page 49 may have baffled you. You may have recognised the person in Fight or Flight, the poem on page 18. Calum's story may have moved you, the way his martial art family wrapped around him, providing guardrails, safety and security in a time of need. It might have been Jen's fight back to reclaim a sense of confidence and self-awareness or the Fight Club feature about the billionaire business of brawling.

The question, I think, is more Kuk Sool *Why?* There are some for whom martial arts may be of little interest and will always remain a mystery. For others, martial arts might manifest positive change, the role it plays in teaching people how to react, respond, remain calm, even remain upright. That's part of the reason this book exists, a story about preservation and celebration, also an act of preserving stories. I think martial arts is about vulnerability, the way we expose ourselves, maybe get to know ourselves and others, even deepen our understanding of self. Martial arts is about building resilience, exposing ourselves voluntarily to the things that we fear. That might be grading or sparring, turning up to train or just the act of living a life with a little less fear. That I believe is the 'Why' behind martial arts. △

'**The bond that links your true family is not one of blood, but of respect and joy in each other's life.**'

Richard Bach, American Writer

# 25

............ YEARS ............

## **ksw**ipswich

The year was 1995. Michael Jordan returned to the NBA, NASA's Galileo spacecraft arrived at Jupiter. There were earthquakes in Japan, a volcano erupted on the island of Montserrat and OJ Simpson was found innocent.

1995 was also the year that John Garrod started his
Kuk Sool Won™ martial arts school in Ipswich. A quarter-century
of moments and experiences, positively influencing the lives of
so many students and families over the years.

The next 25 years will bring changes and challenge to
Kuk Sool Won Ipswich, as well as well as new opportunities.
To never forget the spirit and ethos that has sustained individuals
from all walks of life, in support of personal growth, mental and
physical wellbeing. Where the values of humility and respect
are bestowed, as well as kick ass martial arts skills.

Over the page you'll discover some of those moments,
where photography has that uncanny ability to fix a pivotal
moment that transcends the action and elevates the emotion –
pictures that are testimony to the spirit, ethos and family
that is Kuk Sool Won.

You've nearly completed the book.

Just one last question, before we part company...

It's decision time.

You knew it would come to this.

Do you want to do martial arts?

If you practice martial arts,
keep going, for as long as you can.
If you've not made up your mind,
that's OK, it happens. You need
to go back to page 4 and work
your way through to this page.
Then make a decision.
I'll wait for you here.

If it's a no (for now) that's cool.
We're good.

If it's a yes. That's just great,
you've made my day.

So what are you going to do?

If you've made it this far,
you don't need me to tell you to
maybe go online, type in 'martial
arts', check out YouTube, visit
some sites. Then see what's local.
Make a few calls, speak to a bunch
of people, then attend a couple of
taste & see sessions.

Just before you do, I know I said
one last question... can I ask,
do you like ticking boxes?

# FANCY DOING MARTIAL ARTS? YES ✓

**Grab a pencil, read the questions below and pick 5 that for you capture your 'Why?'**

**Ready?**
**For me, martial arts...**

- ...will make me a badass
- ...will get me out of the house
- ...make me look cool in uniform
- ...help me overcome a fear
- ...make me look like a super-hero
- ...will impress my boyfriend/ girlfriend/partner/mother
- ...might make me feel safer
- ...could help me cope with stuff better
- ...will help me protect myself
- ...will get me fitter
- ...help me meet people
- ...might get me medals and a trophy
- ...will make me believe in something
- ...might help me gain confidence
- ...might just save my life

**Now it's over to you – good luck**

## EPILOGUE

The author's weapons are their words. To be crafted, selected, shaped and deployed. Familiar words, when put into a particular order can stun the reader out of stupor, blast a bias to smithereens or shock and surprise, like a hard slap from your Grandmother.

Why did I decide to write a book about martial arts? To answer that, I'll need to go back to the 1980s. To the era of big hair and even bigger shoulder pads. As a teenager, I grew up in the suburbs of Birmingham. I wasn't academic, didn't play a musical instrument or like reading or writing (ironic isn't it). Sport carried me through the confusion of those early years. Sport, faith and a great bunch of friends. When I was 18, I double-graded under Frank Brennan. From 1979 to 1992, he dominated the KUGB (Karate Union of Great Britain) National Championships. Big deal (him, not me). But perhaps for the first time I discovered a sense of agency, that moment you realise your life is in your hands. At the time, I remember my dad saying something like 'Martial arts is a bit weird.' Here was his son, a talented rugby player who decided to do martial arts. Why?

As a teenager, a book like this didn't exist. If it did, I never found it. You could say that this book represents a message to my younger self, a rather late reply to my dad's question. Also posthumous, he died in 2001. In the spring of 2020, I decided to turn to the 'Why?' behind martial arts. Attempt to create something that somebody might actually want to read. Like an escape capsule from the mundane, create a book that might also entertain, maybe educate or even inspire. Along the journey I discovered that brining an idea into existence is never simple or easy. It takes time, patience, self-discipline, perseverance, commitment and a whole variety of skills as well as other people.

A bit like martial arts in fact.

Now complete, this book is a suggestion that we reframe our bias or preconceived perceptions when it comes to matters of martial arts. It's a story which might fold into the hopes and fears of a teenager somewhere. Actually anyone, anywhere for any number of reasons. Where people have an opportunity to put themselves back together, break down barriers, attract a new generation and bring us together.

On matters of martial arts... It's about so much more than I know. It's also about belting stuff and Hollywood movies.

But you knew that.

**Andrew G Stewart**
**Spring 2021**

## ACKNOWLEDGEMENTS

First, to you, dear reader. Thank you. You may well have thought 'Who the hell does he think he is?' when you first caught sight of the cover title, but you bought the book anyway. I hope I honoured your time and investment.

Sometimes things don't just happen, they get made. That takes time, commitment, grit and graft. In the case of this book, it also took more than just one person.

Grateful thanks to Jon Hatton, for his devilishly good eye for detail. Suzy Powling, whose black belt editorial skills make me sound better than I really am. To Ramsey 'Danger' Dewey, an expert voice on all matters of martial arts – thanks for your voice of reason. Check out his YouTube channel 'Ramsey Dewey'. Special thanks to Sensei Jill Kelly, 6TH Dan and Dylan Gibson, 3RD Dan from Ashington Shotokan Karate Club. Your selection of pictures brought the karate feature to life. To John Garrod, 5TH Dahn Master and Paul Taylor, 6TH Dahn Master. Your patience (with me) is testimony to the art that you've both mastered. Finally, My martial art family and long-standing training partner, Paul Finn.

For many, the 2020/21 pandemic caused great suffering, trauma and loss at so many levels. It also reminded us that to stop and slow down has advantages. I mention, as unusually, I'm indebted to the slow down of lockdown, the 2020/21 Coronacoaster pandemic. Thanks a million. To have time to go a wandering in the long grass, then trip over a martial art side project.

Who would have thought?

**Andrew G Stewart**

P.S. Loui, I had you in mind when I wrote the dedication. We started our martial art journey together. It's why this book ends where it started, with a picture of you and me. And Andrea, thank you. Always.

## MY APPROACH

When it comes to books, every project is different. There are so many variables. Theme, size, shape, tone, typeface, imagery, etc. My ambition, to capture the spirit and ethos behind the subject and not to lose sight of who the book is for. To keep me on track, my maxim: life is short, boredom is failure, no excuses. Honour the subject in the hope of enticing the reader.

Books, like people, have a face. They have a spine, also a back. They can be simple, easy to read or confoundedly complex. Does a cover sell a book? What's more important (than the cover design) is asking a different question: will the book connect with people? That's less about typeface, image selection and colour – that's about relevance, utility and entertainment. On cover title and message, I went for a pejorative approach, designed to spike a response by presenting an unfounded assumption. Mild contempt, with a mea culpa to soften the tone. Why red? It's one of the five elements of traditional Korean culture. Representing energy and life force, also believed to have shamanistic power for warding off evil spirits or bad luck. It's also punchy and stands out when viewed on screen.

On interior design, I've attempted to hold fast to legendary book designer Massimo Vignelli's approach:

*'Establish the grid, the architecture of the book. Like underwear, it's not designed to be revealed. A book, like a film, every sequence and experience needs design, scale, pace, proportion, a visual narrative. The scriptwriter is the author and I'm the director. That's why I get a credit – because the book is mine.'*

## MORE TO GAIN THAN JUST THE GAME

By Dave Courteen (Author)
Designed by Andrew G Stewart

This is not just another book about tennis – it's a story of transformation; where seven narratives capture how sport can change us from the inside out. Moving and motivating first-hand accounts from the world of tennis and beyond. Beautifully designed with stunning photography. The ultimate gift for any tennis fan! Author Dave Courteen is a successful entrepreneur and tennis insider who himself has experienced the transformative power of sport. Large-format book, printed in Italy by one of Europe's leading producers of high-quality books. Foreword by Judy Murray.

*'Great things are possible, and while the route and challenges will be different for each of us, this collection of inspirational stories by Dave Courteen is a catalyst for positive change. And who doesn't want that? I hope you enjoy this book as much as I have.'*

Judy Murray

**www.moretogain.co.uk**
**Available via Amazon, search *More To Gain***

## THE UNBELIEVABLE BOOK

Written designed and produced by Andrew G Stewart

Behind the big blue cover lies the incredible story of adventure, discovery, ancient treasure and a boy on a bench with his grandmother. After 25 years, an innocent question leads to the unveiling of a rather familiar book in unfamiliar circumstances and a question that demanded an answer. Follow a journey that starts in Newcastle, detours to Egypt, includes butter, branding and an unbelievable promise for every reader.

*'It is a lovely object – a big, bold, modern, colourful book, beautifully worked out and impeccably designed'*
*'...you have undoubtedly tackled a gigantic subject. It might have been easier to make it more complicated, but you certainly made the right decision to break it down into manageable sections, telling a compelling story in a simple way. Your writing is excellent, always to the point.'*
*'...it should be made available to every student of theology, as a demonstration that there is always a new way of telling a very old story.'*

Brian Tattersfield, founding partner of Minale Tattersfield

**www.unbelievablebook.uk**

**Available via www.blurb.com, search *The Unbelievable Book Big Blue Edition***

## GENERAL COMMENTS

'Dim Mac' or death touch. There is a bit of a mystery around this one. I'd rather play it safe, so here's the deal. In the words of Master Soon Tae Yang (9TH Degree Black Belt in Taekwondo) 'Attacking pressure points properly can be painful, paralysing or even cause death, depending on the strength and precision of the attack.' Source: https://groups.google.com/forum/#!topic/rec.martial-arts/p695gLsAss0

## REFERENCES

32    [1] Gyaku-zuki, the hardest punch in karate. It does depend on the practitioner, it might be a hammer fist (Tetsui-uchi). Sensei Ikemiyagi Masaaki, 9th Dahn (Okinawa Goju-ryu), demonstrates his power punch, which actually breaks the Makiwara (a padded striking post used as a training tool) on the second strike. You can view at https://www.youtube.com/watch?v=Wx_JsRQ_P9U

[2] Over 180+ martial art styles; Source: https://blackbeltwiki.com/martial-arts-styles

[3] The Global Allure of Karate: https://www.nippon.com/en/views/b06601/

34    [4] Sensei Gichin Funakoshi, founder of Shotokan karate: https://www.shotokankarateonline.com/blog/a-brief-history-of-shotokan-karate/

[5] https://blog.centurymartialarts.com/the-four-main-styles-of-karate-and-their-differences. That said, you could add You could also add Kyokushin and Kenpo

[6] 24 Styles: https://www.thekaratelifestyle.com/what-are-the-types-of-karate/ www.thekaratelifestyle.com

[7] Shotokan, world's most popular karate: https://www.karatebyjesse.com/shotokan-karate-the-4-strengths-of-the-worlds-most-popular-style/

Further reading: Karate-do: *My Way Of Life* by Gichin Funakoshi

58    [8] 'The Better Angels of Our Nature, A History of Violence and Humanity' by Steven Pinker. Penguin Science. ISBN 978-0-141-03464-5

[9] 'When they go low, we go high.' At the Democratic National Convention, Michelle Obama talked about raising her daughters in the spotlight and the importance of rising above negative influences.

[10] Matthew 5:38-41

On violence. Insightful and fascinating article. 'Can There be Virtue in Violence?' Rowland Stout; https://www.cairn.info/revue-internationale-de-philosophie-2006-1-page-323.htm#

60-67    Feature article sources:

UFC: http://ancientolympics.arts.kuleuven.be/eng/TC007cEN.html

Sources: https://www.ancient-origins.net/history-ancient-traditions/pankration-deadly-martial-art-form-ancient-greece-005221 https://www.ufc.com/history-ufc

$4 Billion sale: https://www.nbcsports.com/philadelphia/boxing/ufc-sold-4-billion-white-stays-run-promotion

The fight game reloaded: how MMA and UFC conquered the world; UFC article by Andy Bull (Guardian, Fri 4 Mar 2016): https://www.theguardian.com/sport/2016/mar/04/the-fight-game-reloaded-how-mma-conquered-world-ufc

UFC 189 / Robbie Lawler and former UFC welterweight fighter/titile contender Rory Macdonald. It's widely regarded as being the greatest MMA fight of all time· according to https://bleacherreport.com/articles/2521190-robbie-lawler-vs-rory-macdonald-mmas-fight-of-the-year-so-far

76 -85    There are volumes of text books that dive deeply into the history, theory, philosophy and application of Kuk Sool Won. For further information, visit www.kuksoolwon.com

78    [11] http://www.kuksoolwon.com/site/founder Kuk Sool Won, Textbook Volume 2, Letter from the Grandmaster.

[12] https://www.kuksoolwonofkingslynn.co.uk/history/4590383209

[13] https://www.kuksoolwonofkingslynn.co.uk/history/4590383209

80    [14] 'The Historical Sociology of Japanese Martial Arts' by Raul Sanchez Garcia. ISBN 978-1-138-57169-3

## PICTURE CREDITS

## LEGALS

# WHY EVERYTHING YOU KNOW ABOUT MARTIAL ARTS IS WRONG*

→ A2 & A3 Poster ideas.
Visit www.unbelievablebook.uk

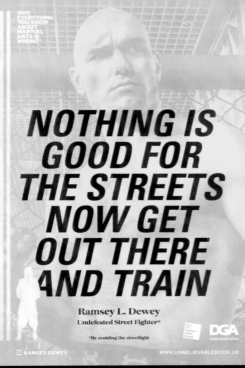

## BANGING THE DRUM

Somebody asked me 'So what's your plan, when it comes to turning to a big question? How do you answer it, then share 'it' with the world?'

Here's my answer. Write the best damn story you can. Wrestle with it, dance with it, reject and return to it. Shape it, reduce and capture it – if you can. If it's easy, you're not trying hard enough. You're going to hate the piece and love the piece. Go close, then view from afar. Think on it and play with it. Look at it through the eyes of a child. Write one word at a time. One sentence at a time and build the narrative. Research and critique it. Crush it. What ever remains, that's the foundation. Then dress it, add colour, scale, pace, tone and shape. Like a play, a bit of theatre. Create one set, one movement, one act at a time. Always be grateful that the question came knocking at your door. It might have gone else where. So honour the question.

Over time, I've been commissioned to help people articulate and tell stories. In digital and print. Stories that aim to capture and hold someone's attention. To encourage people to do something, feel something, change something, buy something or be a part of something. I'm lucky. I've picked up a particular set of skills this past 30 years. Also met a bunch of highly competent contributors who have pitched in on this thing that you now hold in your hands. On the answer, for me it turned out to be a book. It might be different for you. Ohhh, and there are no guarantees on the outcome. It's the journey. Your journey will look different to mine. Mine looked something like this:

01: Make sure you're asking the right questions.
02: Know your audience: is it just for you, or for others too?
03: Write the best damn story you can.
04: Design the best damn book you can.
05: Finish what you started. Simon Coupe, my buddy said that.
06: Share what you've created. Send to highly-competent people who have dedicated their lives to the subject you've written about. Invite contributors. Ask humbly for honest opinion to gauge utility. It's all data. It might stop here.
07: Take the feedback. Revisit the questions, it'll only make it stronger. Reshape and recreate then lock down. Just not in a pandemic way.
08: Create a platform, the best damn website you can with the tools and funds available. In a time-frame that doesn't kill momentum.
09: Reflect. De-bullsh*t any aspect. It's one thing embarrassing yourself. You don't want to broadcast bluff and bullsh*t globally. Prepare to launch.
10: Curate the sound-bites, the endorser's feedback, ready to deploy via social channels. Package the eye-candy, to entice the viewer, stop the scroll and *maybe* convert the 'click'.
11: Take a breath. Dial down anticipation, in the hope of expectation.
12: Review the process, consider fulfilment, scalability, the transactional journey, the hoped-for exchange. Set a margin. Go lower in the hope to increase traction and velocity.
13: Unlucky (for some). You need a bit of luck for 'it' to work. A lot of luck.
14: Deploy. Push the button.

## BANG THE DRUM

What happens next? The drum beat has a rhythm, it's not a one-off event.
Maintain visibility on digital channels.
Reach out to identified audiences and influential gatekeepers.
Prepare to put a book into an envelope and post.

When you're done, go and answer another question.

## Connect with me on social
### Search #unbelievablebook

 **unbelievablebook**

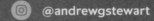 **@andrewgstewart**

 **@believable_book**

→ **Snapshot:** social marketing, outreach, response and research. Everything is data.

↓ **Endorser pack:** Limited to just 20 packs. Sent to high-level martial art luminaries, coaches and commentators to gauge utility and response.

A LOAD
OF HONG
KONG
PHOOEY

→ **Social adverts and sound-bites.** The endorser's take. Cast broadly into the sea of digital. With a #line that links to the landing net, the transactional website. The shop. The place of exchange. Will anyone buy the book? Will I get any likes or shares? Don't be needy. Needy is when people are short on water, food, shelter and protection. If the book lands well, the idea, it should sell itself. Or it won't. You finished what you started. Be content with that.

WHY
EVERYTHING
YOU KNOW
ABOUT
MARTIAL
ARTS IS
WRONG*

▶ PRE-ORDER NOW
LINK BELOW

'There are thousands of books on martial arts out there, few cut through the noise and cliché in such a succinct and intriguing way'

GIOVANNI SOFFIETTO
FOUNDER & CEO
BRITISH MARTIAL ARTS & BOXING ASSOCIATION

→ **Everything is data.** You can never do too much research. Just don't get lost in it or lose yourself along the way. Leave a thread that leads back to where you started. You'll discover that nothing is new. Everything is a remix. Don't die in pursuit of the original or perfect. Leave that to the geniuses. If you are one, a genius, remember that you're not one. You've been visited by a 'Genius', true creativity is divinely inspired. Either way, creativity is hard graft. Stop talking about what you're going to do... Start doing it!

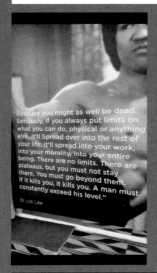

"Because you might as well be dead. Seriously, if you always put limits on what you can do, physical or anything else, it'll Spread over into the rest of your life! It'll spread into your work, into your morality. Into your entire being. There are no limits. There are plateaus, but you must not stay there, You must go beyond them. If it kills you, it kills you. A man must constantly exceed his level."

Bruce Lee

FIGHT
CLUB

↘ **Remember to play with the idea.** Remain curious. There are different answers to the same question, so be wary of the easy ones that shout back at you. If you can, be generous. Give stuff away. If the heart behind what you do is honest and truthful, in so far as the stories you create, people will catch it. They might celebrate it. They might even buy into it.

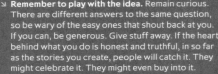

NOTHING IS
GOOD FOR
THE STREETS
NOW GET
OUT THERE
AND TRAIN

Ramsey L. Dewey
Undefeated Street Fighter*

"By avoiding the streetlight"

DGA

"

He who knows all the answers has not been asked all the questions.

CONFUCIUS

"

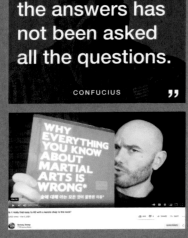

WHY
EVERYTHING
YOU KNOW
ABOUT
MARTIAL
ARTS IS
WRONG*